THE COLOR OF THEIR SKIN
Education and Race in Richmond, Virginia, 1954–89

Carter G. Woodson Institute Series in Black Studies

Armstead L. Robinson
General Editor

THE COLOR OF THEIR SKIN

Education and Race in Richmond, Virginia

1954-89

by Robert A. Pratt

University Press of Virginia

Charlottesville and London

THE UNIVERSITY PRESS OF VIRGINIA

Copyright ©1992 by the Rector and Visitors
of the University of Virginia

First published 1992

Library of Congress Cataloging-in-Publication Data

Pratt, Robert A., 1958–
    The color of their skin : education and race in Richmond,
Virginia, 1954–89 / by Robert A. Pratt.
        p.   cm. — (Carter G. Woodson Institute series in Black
    studies)
    Includes bibliographical references (p.) and index.
    ISBN 0-8139-1372-1
    1. School integration—Virginia—Richmond—History. I. Title.
II. Series.
    LC214.323.R53P63   1992
    370.19'342—dc20   91-35590
                                                                          CIP

Printed in the United States of America

For My Grandmothers

Rosa Clark Pratt

and

Naomi Gaines Taylor

Separate school children by wealth and the result is class misunderstanding and hatred. Separate by race and the result is war. Separate them by color and they grow up without learning the tremendous truth that it is impossible to judge the mind of a man by the color of his face. Is there any truth that America needs to learn more?

W. E. B. DuBois, *Crisis,* November 1910

Contents

Preface

This study examines one southern city's prolonged, thirty–five year resistance to school desegregation. It is the story of school desegregation in Richmond, Virginia. It shows how Richmond's "passive" resistance succeeded where Virginia's "massive" resistance had failed. Although the era of "massive resistance" witnessed school closings in several Virginia localities, Richmond's public schools remained open throughout the entire crisis—open, but segregated. By the time the first blacks applied to all-white schools in 1958, school officials, acting under state law, were already operating a carefully crafted policy aimed at avoiding integration without having to resort to a flagrant display of local defiance, which, as the demise of massive resistance had so clearly shown, could not be sustained indefinitely. Rather, so as not to aggravate the prejudices of whites who simply were not yet willing to send their children to school with blacks, community leaders and school officials dragged their feet, hoping to bury school desegregation under the weight of gradual compliance. Though this policy of passive resistance would ultimately crumble under the pressure of an activist judiciary, it stayed in place long enough to allow uncompromising whites to achieve their objectives. As the pressure to desegregate the schools increased, whites withdrew from the city's school system in ever–growing numbers. The result was resegregation within the city's schools. Richmond's school population, 57 percent white in 1954, would be 88 percent black thirty–five years later.

Because Richmond's city officials and school administrators showed no inclination to move beyond their policy of token integration, it was incumbent upon local black attorneys to initiate all legal action aimed at ending Richmond's history of dual education. Since state and city officials were determined to make blacks exhaust all legal remedies before segregated schools were dismantled, Richmond's black attorneys had to push the school desegregation issue forward so that the courts would be forced to take a clear and unequivocal position on school desegregation once and for all. In this way, black activism served as the primary catalyst for the demise of state–sanctioned segregation in Richmond's public schools. Eventually, though, de jure segregation would be replaced by de facto segregation as increasing numbers of whites abandoned the city schools in favor of private or suburban public schools with predominantly white or all-white enrollments.

In many ways, the story of Richmond is representative of those many urban localities throughout the country where efforts to desegregate the public schools have often been met with fierce opposition, increased racial separation and hostility, and a gradual erosion of support for public education. Some historians, such as Lino Graglia and Raymond Wolters, whose views on the subject are very much different from my own, will no doubt conclude that public education in Richmond might have been spared such a massive loss of white middle–class (and increasingly black middle–class) support had the courts and black activists been content to allow school integration to occur gradually and incrementally so that the process would not have been so immediately offensive and disruptive to whites' social customs. Yet, it is clear that in the absence of aggressive judicial action and black activism, Richmond's schools would have remained racially segregated. Virginia's brief history of massive resistance had clearly demonstrated not only that local white officials would not voluntarily implement school desegregation policies but that they would use every conceivable means to resist the courts' desegregation rulings. In contrast to this intransigence, the principled decisions of Richmond's district court judge, the courage of the black children and their parents who demanded desegregation, and the tenacity of black attorneys stand out in this story as examples of honor and fidelity to the meaning of *Brown,* even if the result was the white abandonment of the public schools.

The story of Richmond, Virginia, has implications far beyond that city or state. School desegregation there was the centerpiece of a series of judicial decisions that have helped to structure public education across the United States, as Richmond, in 1973, was the first city where the issue of metropolitan school consolidation—merging a city's school system with neighboring suburban school districts, usually to create or maintain a more even racial balance—was debated before the United States Supreme Court. (In *Richmond v. Virginia State Board of Education,* a divided Court left the issue unresolved. The following year, in *Milliken v. Bradley,* the Court, in a five–to–four decision, overturned a district–court plan that would have merged Detroit's schools with fifty–three predominantly white suburban school districts.) Richmond's story is especially illuminating because it reveals many of the complexities and pitfalls inherent in attempting to desegregate a city's schools within a metropolitan context. Years of foot–dragging in the implementation of school desegregation not only facilitated and encouraged white migration out of the cities into the neighboring suburbs, it also allowed the conservative leadership additional time to mobilize its forces and gradually alter the composition of the federal courts, especially the United States Supreme Court. As busing became increasingly unpopular, white resistance to "forced desegregation" intensified, a sentiment clearly reflected in President Richard M. Nixon's administration and in his appointments to the Supreme Court. By the early 1970s it was apparent that a revitalized conservative consensus was taking shape, and school desegregation was no longer the priority it once had been. One cannot help but speculate that if the NAACP and other civil rights groups had been able to anticipate such a change of direction in regard to school desegregation policy, they might have pursued metropolitan consolidation sooner while the federal courts were more kindly disposed toward petitioners seeking equal justice. Whereas the Warren Court of 1954 might eventually have ruled in favor of metropolitan school consolidation, the much more conservative Burger Court, ruling in *Milliken v. Bradley* twenty years later, did not. (It is significant to note that four of those voting with the majority—Chief Justice Warren E. Burger, Justices Harry A. Blackmun, Lewis F. Powell, Jr., and William H. Rehnquist—were Nixon appointees. The fifth justice, Potter Stewart, was appointed by Eisenhower.) In the fifteen years since *Milliken,* the Supreme Court has become even more conservative under the Reagan and Bush administrations, and it is highly unlikely that the current Supreme Court, whose influence will be felt well into the next century, will rethink its position on metropolitan desegregation. It is a curious irony indeed that the public schools of rural Prince Edward County, Virginia, whose doors were closed from 1959 to 1964 in brazen defiance of the *Brown* decision, are today more desegregated than those of Richmond, where the school doors remained open.

Despite the significant role the courts played, it is the individual acts of courage and defiance that stand out as the most powerful images in Richmond's story: the two city engineers who, on their hands and knees, measured the distance from a black family's home to prove that they lived closer to a black school than to a white one; Governor Linwood Holton's personal decision to escort his daughter to a predominantly black school on the first day of classes in 1970; the thousands of white parents and students who took to the streets to protest Judge Merhige's rulings; and, the decision of a black-controlled school board to discontinue busing after sixteen years of trying to achieve desegregation.

Despite the furor over attempts at school desegregation, Richmond's blacks did not give up on public education; instead, they made the necessary adjustments and worked to ensure that their children's educational needs were met, even in the absence of a solid white middle–class base.

What follows is a portrait of education's survival in the midst of desegregation's failure. Fortunately for the black and white students who remain in Richmond's public school system, the success of one did not necessarily hinge upon the success of the other.

Acknowledgments

This book grew out of the very first seminar paper I wrote as a graduate student at the University of Virginia in the fall of 1980. My professor for that course, Paul M. Gaston, was also my major advisor, and it was he who suggested the topic. With his constant support and encouragement, I was able to expand that paper into my doctoral thesis. After several years of extensive revisions, here it is, at long last, in published form.

Many people helped to make this book possible, and I have incurred many debts along the way. My greatest debts are to Professors Paul M. Gaston and Armstead L. Robinson, both of whom were initially my mentors, but over the years have become very close friends. It was Paul who provided me with professional guidance and moral support during the early (and sometimes depressing) years of graduate study at the University of Virginia, and it was he who tried to make me feel comfortable in what was often for me an uncomfortable environment. Always gracious in demeanor but never sparing in criticism, he scrutinized my work with a trained scholar's eye and helped me to understand the difference between recording history and learning from it. Armstead Robinson, who joined the history faculty in 1980 and shortly thereafter was appointed director of the newly created Carter G. Woodson Institute for Afro-American and African Studies, immediately became both mentor and friend. He was able to tap into a reservoir of self-confidence that I had forgotten existed, and he demonstrated by example the potential I hoped to realize one day. In our daily conversations about the manuscript in particular and the profession in general, Armstead, more than anyone else, helped me to understand that the race is not given to the swift, nor to the strong, but to him who endureth to the end. Praise be to the Almighty—I have endured.

I wish also to acknowledge Professors Edward L. Ayers, Robert D. Cross, Joseph C. Miller, and Waldo E. Martin, Jr., for their numerous contributions to this project. Each of them read either portions or all of the manuscript at various stages, and I hope the final product positively reflects their collective contributions. Thanks also to Professor William S. McFeely, my colleague at the University of Georgia, for his insightful suggestions and moral support. Other colleagues who offered their assistance are Professors Emory Thomas, Numan Bartley, Lester Stephens, F. N. Boney, Carl Vipperman, John H. Morrow, Jr., Lee Kennett, and Charles Wynes. I am grateful to them all. I reserve a special thanks for Professor Harold E. Greer, Jr., one of my professors at Virginia Commonwealth University, who has been instrumental in helping to shape my career thus far. It was because of his encouragement that I applied for, and subsequently won, a Danforth Fellowship that financed most of my graduate education. He is a remarkable man with a courageous spirit, and I am proud to call him friend.

I gratefully acknowledge the Carter G. Woodson Institute for its financial and technical assistance while I was completing my dissertation. Professor William E. Jackson, associate director of the institute, always managed to find travel money for me during my summer research trips. In addition, I had unlimited access to a word processor, a copying machine, and numerous other facilities, as well as the expert technical assistance of Mary Rose, the institute's computer specialist, and Gail Shirley, the administrative secretary. In addition to the tangible benefits, the Woodson Institute fostered a mutually reinforcing community of scholars who were eager to create an environment that appreciated and encouraged cultural diversity. My five-year affiliation with the Woodson Institute was both challenging and gratifying, and I am grateful to those who made it happen.

I wish to thank especially the following organizations whose financial support, in the form of research grants and fellowships, helped make this book possible: the Danforth Foundation, the Virginia Council of Higher Education, the University of Georgia's Humanities Center and Office of the Vice-President for Research, the Virginia Foundation for the Humanities and Public Policy, the Virginia Historical Society, and the Spencer Foundation. For their research assistance, I wish to thank the Valentine Museum, the Richmond Public Library, the Richmond School Board, the Richmond Department of Planning, the Virginia State Library, and the libraries at Virginia Commonwealth University and the University of Virginia. I wish to thank the Virginia Historical Society for making certain manuscript collections available, and I wish to thank the Valentine Museum, especially Gregg Kimball, and the Richmond Newspapers for supplying the photographs. I also wish to thank Shirley Callihan of the Richmond Public Schools for her assistance in helping me to locate school board documents.

I wanted to paint a personal, as well as a scholarly, portrait of Richmond, Virginia, between 1954 and 1989, and this simply would not have been possible without the willingness of many individuals to share with me their personal experiences. Realizing the limitations inherent in oral history, and understanding that memory is often frail (and sometimes convenient), I have nonetheless relied heavily upon personal interviews, primarily because I believe they lend both immediacy and authenticity to this study. With only one exception—James J. Kilpatrick—every person I contacted agreed to an interview. I think it is fair to say that the story I wanted to tell would not have materialized without their assistance, and I hereby gratefully acknowledge them, in alphabetical order, for their generous contributions to this book: Zeke Allison, Alice R. Calloway, Herman L. Carter, Jr., Charles Cox, Virginia Crockford, Virginius Dabney, Dr. Francis M. Foster, Sr., Harold E. and Laura Greer, Arnold R. Henderson, Jr., Oliver W. Hill, Linwood Holton, Richard C. Hunter, George H. Johnson, Sabrina C. Johnson, George L. Jones, Melvin Law, Nathaniel Lee, Henry L. Marsh, III, Robert R. Merhige, Jr., Lewis F. Powell, Jr., Angelo Setien, Samuel W. Tucker, James W. Tyler, Bernard C. and Marsha Vandervall, Roy A. West, and Kenneth E. Whitlock, Jr.

Finally, I wish to thank my parents, Barbara and Robert E. Pratt, who have helped me in more ways than I can count. They have given me as much support as any parents could give a son, and I have tried my very best to make them proud. To my darling wife, Anita, whose patience, love, and encouragement kept me going during some of my most difficult days, I hope you know that I thank you and I love you, and that I could not have made it without you. You have been my constant companion and my best friend. Last, but certainly not least, I wish to thank my grandmother, Naomi Gaines Taylor, whose enduring love and affection have sustained me since the earliest rocking of my cradle. She is, without a doubt, my guiding spirit and my greatest inspiration. It is to her, and to the memory of my paternal grandmother, Rosa Clark Pratt, that this book is dedicated.

THE COLOR OF THEIR SKIN
Education and Race in Richmond, Virginia, 1954–89

I have a dream that my four little children will one day live in a nation where they will not be judged by the color of their skin, but by the content of their character.

Rev. Dr. Martin Luther King, Jr.
March on Washington
August 28, 1963

ONE

A Shameful Legacy

In the first instance, I think most of us would agree that to "segregate" is to "stigmatize," however much we may try to rationalize it. . . . For we all know that segregation is practically always initiated by the whites, and initiated on the basis that Negroes are inferior and undesirable. . . . In the second instance, the separate school is generally uneconomical, and frequently financially burdensome. . . . Consequently, where sufficient funds are not available to support decent schools for both whites and Negroes, and even in many cases where they are sufficient, it is the Negro school that suffers, and there is very little that is done about it. Those who argue that the separate school with equal facilities is superior to the mixed school with prejudice should know that the separate school, or separate anything, with equal facilities is a fiction.

—Charles H. Thompson, 1935

On Monday, May 17, 1954, the United States Supreme Court handed down its historic school desegregation decision in *Brown v. Board of Education*.[1] The Court ruled unanimously that segregation of black and white children in public schools was unconstitutional and had to end. The policy of "separate but equal," as enunciated by the Court in *Plessy v. Ferguson* in 1896, was dead at last. As the bombing of Pearl Harbor was to the entire nation, so the *Brown* decision was to the white South—an assault to be recorded for posterity as yet another event that would live in infamy.

All across the region angry white politicians reacted sharply to the Court's ruling, and, as was customary in such matters, Virginia's politicians took the lead. Senator Harry F. Byrd described the decision as the "most serious blow that has been struck against the rights of the States in a matter vitally affecting their authority and welfare." Byrd stated further that "the decision will be deplored by millions of Americans, and instead of promoting the education of our children, it is my belief it will have the opposite effect in many areas of the country. In Virginia, we are now facing a crisis of the first magnitude." Attorney General J. Lindsay Almond said that he was also "convinced that integration of the races in the school system will set education back, and that the decision is a drastic blow at the right of the sovereign State to maintain its own public school system without interference from the Federal government." Congressman William M. Tuck said that he was unable "to employ words to express my chagrin over the decision." The Richmond *Times-Dispatch* reported that "officials of some states already are on record as saying they will close the schools rather than permit them to be operated with Negro and white pupils in the same classrooms."[2]

Although not a single Virginia politician supported *Brown,* not all were as enraged as Senator Byrd. Some, like Governor Thomas B. Stanley, at least urged citizens to be calm. "This news today," Stanley remarked, "calls for cool heads, calm study and sound judgement. I am sure the people of Virginia and their elected representatives can find the right solution. I hope all will cooperate to afford this opportunity for the careful development of a program which will be in the best interest of the entire citizenship." Republican state Senator Ted Dalton urged Governor Stanley to appoint a "nonpartisan, biracial commission" that could study the situation and offer a sound solution. Dalton agreed that there should be "no hasty or precipitate action," but felt that the commission should be put together as soon as possible.[3]

Whatever the tone of their initial statements, most Virginia politicians agreed that the Court's ruling was an unwarranted intrusion upon state's rights and that the end result would be a decline rather than an improvement in the standards of education. For the moment, however, their only consolation was the realization that actual implementation of school desegregation would not occur immediately. For the Court to hand down such a far-reaching decision was one thing; to enforce it was quite another. Nowhere was this sentiment better reflected than in Richmond's two major newspapers, the *Times-Dispatch* and the *News Leader.* On the day after the ruling the *Times-Dispatch* had these comments:

> We had hoped that the court would uphold the "separate but equal" doctrine, but since it did not do so, this is a time for calm and unhysterical appraisal of the situation by the officials and people of Virginia and the other 16 states where segregated schools are now required. . . . An important consideration in this whole discussion is the undoubted fact that full integration throughout the 17 states will take a long time. A vast number of local and individual problems will have to be worked out, and each of the separate localities and States must adjust to the new dispensations. This could easily take a decade or two. . . . So despite yesterday's ruling by the court, epoch-making though it

is, segregation in the public schools of the South is not about to be eliminated. Final achievement of that objective is years, perhaps many years, in the future.[4]

On the same day the Richmond *News Leader* commented:

To bring the two races together in the social intimacy of a classroom will not come easily to the South. This newspaper, as its readers know, believes in segregated schools. We believe also in abiding by the law.

However, if the court would consent to a more moderate program of integration, the prospect of preserving public education in the South would be immeasurably improved. . . . But the court should not misunderstand or underestimate the depth of resentment this opinion will create among a people who feel they have been wrongly imposed upon.[5]

The newspapers' predictions were ominous, for although such pronouncements were initially veiled in a veneer of gradual compliance, suggestions of discord were already beginning to appear.

Understandably, the black community had a totally different perception of and response to the Court's desegregation order. State officials of the NAACP hailed the decision as "a landmark comparable to the Declaration of Independence." Robert Johnson, a history professor at Virginia Union University, said that "this is a most exciting moment. I haven't seen such collective emotion since the day Roosevelt died. A lot of us haven't been breathing for the past nine months. But today the students reacted as if a heavy burden had been lifted from their shoulders. They see a new world opening up for them and those that follow them."[6]

No one could have been more pleased with the decision than Thurgood Marshall, the NAACP's star advocate, who had been in the forefront of the struggle from the very beginning. Marshall, who had by now distinguished himself as the most prominent black attorney in the country and whose name had become synonymous with civil rights, said that the *Brown* decision was "the greatest victory we ever had. . . . The thing that is gratifying to me is that it was unanimous and on our side and it settles once and for all this question of separate but equal." Although delighted with the decision, Marshall was understandably cautious about participating in a victory celebration that might be premature, for he correctly surmised that it would take some time for Southern legislators to fall in step with the federal judiciary, and until that happened the issue was far from settled. When asked about the possibility of defiance in the South, Marshall promised that if any state tried to sidestep the Supreme Court ruling, the NAACP would gladly return to court. "If they try it in the morning, we'll have them in court the next morning—or possibly that same afternoon."[7] Marshall's suspicions would soon be confirmed.

On June 20, twenty legislators from Southside Virginia met in Peters-

burg under the leadership of state Senator Garland Gray to declare themselves "unalterably opposed" to school integration. By now it was evident
that the vast majority of Virginia's politicians unswervingly adhered to the
provision in Section 140 of the state constitution which stated that "white
and colored children shall not be taught in the same school."[8] The few
whites who conscientiously believed in integration were reluctant to say so
publicly for fear of being socially ostracized and branded as traitors and
nigger lovers. Further, Virginia politicians knew that to challenge the
powerful Byrd organization on such a crucial issue would be tantamount to
political suicide. Not surprisingly, on June 25, only five short weeks after
his moderate statement calling for "calm study and sound judgement,"
Governor Stanley declared: "I shall use every legal means at my command
to continue segregated schools in Virginia."[9] The fragile spirit of cooperation had suddenly given way to a mood of defiance. What would come to
be known as massive resistance had begun.

On August 23 Governor Stanley appointed a thirty-two member, all-
white, legislative commission to study the problems created by the Court's
decision and to formulate a course of action. Although each district was
represented by at least two commission members, the greatest weight was
given to those districts with the highest black population percentages, so
that the rural, black-belt, Byrd-supported Democrats dominated the commission.[10] Virginia politicians considered this to be a fair arrangement
since Southside Virginia, which had the highest proportion of black
residents, would be the area most affected by the Court ruling. And
because blacks made up such a large percentage of the population in the
Southside region, it was correctly surmised that this area would provide the
most fertile breeding ground for staunch segregationists. When the commission's members met for the first time on September 13 they elected as
chairman state Senator Garland Gray, who had led the anti-integration
meeting in Petersburg a few months earlier.[11]

Before the Gray Commission could submit its recommendations to the
governor, the Supreme Court, on May 31, 1955, delivered its implementation decision. This second *Brown* decision, however, refrained from fixing
deadlines or uniform conditions for school desegregation. Instead, it placed
the burden of implementation on the district courts and offered only the
vague command that racial segregation in public schools should be eliminated "with all deliberate speed."[12] The ambiguity of that phrase would
permit much more deliberation than speed. In fact, the absence of specific
guidelines not only afforded Southern politicians the opportunity to delay
indefinitely actual implementation but, more important, gave them extra
time to formulate a strategy that would evade the Court's ruling altogether.
By the time *Brown* II was delivered, the seeds of bitter defiance had already
begun to germinate, and most Virginia politicians were now steadfastly

committed to maintaining segregated schools throughout the state, even if it meant a direct confrontation with the federal courts.

After more than a year of deliberation, the Gray Commission finally submitted its report on November 11, 1955. Despite their vehement opposition to school desegregation, the members of the commission considered it imprudent, at least for the moment, to challenge directly the authority of the Supreme Court and believed that a moderate course of action would be more judicious. The Gray Plan, as it came to be called, made two basic recommendations. First, it proposed that local school boards be given broad discretion on the issue of pupil assignment and that their criteria consist of "such factors as availability of facilities, health, aptitude of the child and the availability of transportation." Further, the commission added that "assignment would be based upon the welfare and best interests of all other pupils attending a particular school."[13] This phase of the plan would be facilitated by the creation of a state Pupil Placement Board to which local school districts were to refer all Negro applications to white schools. Second, in order to ensure that no child be forced to attend an integrated school, the commission recommended that a system of tuition grants from public funds be established to aid any pupil who preferred to attend a segregated private school rather than an integrated public one. To facilitate this phase of the plan, the commission urged the General Assembly to amend the compulsory attendance law so that no child would be required to attend an integrated school.[14] Although this plan, moderate in retrospect, urged only that students not be forced to attend integrated schools and tacitly conceded that some integration would be tolerated, commission members were convinced that extensive application procedures and local custom would effectively keep school integration at token levels. Hence, the essentials of the dual school system would be preserved.

Despite its potential effectiveness, the Gray Plan generally displeased most of Virginia's conservatives, who advocated a more radical course of action. This conservative movement gained increasing momentum following the referendum in which Virginians overwhelmingly endorsed the concept of tuition grants to private schools, and it received an added impetus in the early months of 1956 when the dynamic young editor of the Richmond *News Leader* rose to prominence. James Jackson Kilpatrick, Jr., one of the South's most articulate segregation spokesmen, used his inflammatory editorials to provide constitutional and intellectual justification for massive resistance as he sought to change its overall character from something ignominious to something noble. J. Harvie Wilkinson notes that Kilpatrick "had learned Virginian modes of thought, and he seldom failed to cast his editorial appeals in an irresistibly Virginian way. He was easily one of the most gifted phrasemakers of the national press."[15]

A staunch defender of both segregation and state's rights, Kilpatrick revived the doctrine of "interposition," which supposedly endowed the state with the authority to resist, and, if necessary, to nullify any federal ruling it considered unconstitutional. First used in 1798 by Thomas Jefferson and James Madison in response to the Alien and Sedition Acts, and again in the 1830s by John C. Calhoun during South Carolina's nullification crisis over protective tariffs, interposition became a popular, if not always an effective, strategy among ardent defenders of state's rights. For over two months the editorial page of the Richmond *News Leader* was devoted to interposition.[16] Kilpatrick's editorials appear to have been convincing, for by early 1956 he had endeared himself to millions of white Southerners as one of the chief architects of massive resistance to school desegregation.[17] In fact, his impassioned argument in favor of segregation (which he would later publish in a book entitled *The Southern Case for School Segregation*) was of such intensity that the 1956 session of the General Assembly voted overwhelmingly to adopt an interposition resolution "to resist this illegal encroachment upon our sovereign powers, and to urge upon our sister States, whose authority over their own most cherished powers may next be imperilled, their prompt and deliberate efforts to check this further encroachment by the Supreme Court, through judicial legislation, upon the reserved powers of the States."[18]

Once the General Assembly adopted interposition in early 1956, the Gray Plan, which stressed local option and held out the possibility for some integration, was immediately rejected. Byrd forces saw the interposition resolution, along with the outcome of the tuition grant referendum (which Byrd himself was primarily responsible for initiating), as a clear mandate for total resistance to school desegregation. On February 24, Senator Byrd issued a statement from Washington, D.C., in which he first used the phrase *massive resistance*: "If we can organize the Southern States for massive resistance to this order I think that in time the rest of the country will realize that racial integration is not going to be accepted in the South." Virginia had now thrown down the gauntlet.[19]

On March 5 a constitutional convention of forty delegates (one from each of the state's forty senatorial districts) convened in Richmond to carry out the mandate of the tuition-grant referendum. The delegates unanimously amended Section 141 of the state constitution to legalize tuition grants to pupils attending "public and nonsectarian private schools and institutions of learning." The local-option provision, offered by H. D. Dawbarn of Waynesboro, was rejected by the convention's privileges and elections committee. A resolution supporting the doctrine of interposition was adopted by a vote of thirty-five to three. And, one week later, Senator Byrd was one of the leading sponsors of the "Southern Manifesto," signed by 101 Southern members of Congress, and introduced in the House and Senate on March 12, which attacked the Supreme Court's desegregation ruling "as a clear abuse of judicial power" and commended "those states which have declared the intention to resist forced integration by any lawful means."[20] Massive resistance was on the move.

During the summer of 1956, the NAACP filed desegregation suits against the school boards in Arlington, Norfolk, Newport News, and Charlottesville. In an attempt to formulate an effective counterattack, the leaders of the massive–resistance movement, including Governor Stanley, state Senator Gray, and U.S. representatives Tuck and Abbitt, held a secret meeting with Senator Byrd in Washington, D.C. Subsequent meetings were held throughout the summer in Governor Stanley's Richmond offices. In the course of these meetings all agreed that there would be no retreat from massive resistance. They then decided to hold a special session of the General Assembly in mid-August for the purpose of drafting legislation that would make school integration virtually impossible.[21]

On August 27, 1956, the members of the Virginia legislature convened for the expressed purpose of defeating the Supreme Court's desegregation decree. The Byrd forces introduced a thirteen-bill anti-integration package to the legislature for consideration. Together, these bills constituted what would later become known as the Stanley Plan. First proposed was the creation of a pupil placement board, which would function as a statewide agency vested with the authority to assign all students to public schools in Virginia and to handle all requests for transfer. Although not explicitly stated, it was clearly understood that the primary function of the Pupil Placement Board was to maintain segregated schools. If the NAACP disputed the placement board's authority and challenged its constitutional-ity in federal courts, as it surely would, the courts would order the school district to admit black pupils to white schools. To prevent that from happening, the legislators passed a law requiring the governor to close any school threatened with integration and to remove it from the public school system. He was then to attempt to reopen that school on a segregated basis by encouraging blacks to withdraw their applications voluntarily. If reor-ganization proved unsuccessful, and if, for some reason, a local school decided to open on an integrated basis, whether voluntarily or under court order, state funds were to be cut off from all the schools in that district. Such a loss of funding would have been disastrous for all but a handful of cities and counties. Finally, the massive–resistance laws authorized the state to provide private–school tuition grants from public funds to parents in any district where the public schools were closed to prevent integration.[22] The General Assembly had fulfilled its mission, for it was now highly unlikely that any school integration would occur in the Old Dominion.

The massive–resistance legislation was not unanimously adopted by the General Assembly. A few moderates dissented from the extremist majority, but the emotion surrounding school integration had reached such intensity

that these brave souls represented an ever-dwindling and a most conspicuous minority. Two major political figures, Democratic state Senator
Armistead L. Boothe and Republican state Senator Ted Dalton made a
valiant last-ditch effort to insert a local–option provision in the fund cutoff
measure so that localities could avoid the more extreme consequences of
the Stanley Plan. But the adoption of interposition had sounded the death
knell for local option, and those moderates seeking to resurrect it clashed
with the stalwarts of the Byrd organization, such as state Senator Mills E.
Godwin, Jr. A belligerent defender of segregation, Godwin claimed that
"integration is the key which opens the door to the inevitable destruction of
our free public schools" and that "integration, however slight, anywhere in
Virginia would be a cancer eating at the very life blood of our public school
system."[23] Clearly, the moderates could not prevail against such bitter
defiance. The voices of reason were completely muffled by the sound and
the fury of segregationist rhetoric.

In the twenty-seven day session, Virginia's legislators passed a total of
twenty-three acts designed to prevent the implementation of *Brown*. Seven
of the acts were aimed at the NAACP. The NAACP was in the forefront of
the school desegregation drive, and it filed more suits in Virginia than in
any other state. There was a widespread feeling among Virginia's legislators that the NAACP was primarily responsible for most of the desegregation litigation throughout the South. Few white Virginians were openly
sympathetic to the black struggle for equality, and the NAACP, the organization that best symbolized that struggle, was the frequent target of segregationists, who regarded it as sinister and Communist-inspired. The
General Assembly hoped that school desegregation would be defeated if the
NAACP's activities were restricted. These anti-NAACP acts fell into two
major categories. One dealt with the illegal practice of law, while the other
required all organizations that raised money for racial litigation to register
with the State Corporation Commission and to disclose the names of all
contributors, officers, members, and employees.[24]

The General Assembly also created two joint committees to investigate
the enforcement of these laws and to monitor the activities of organizations
that encouraged racial litigation. The Committee on Law Reform and
Racial Activities, chaired by Delegate James M. Thomson of Alexandria,
and the Committee on Offenses against the Administration of Justice,
chaired by Delegate John B. Boatwright of Buckingham County, began
their intensive investigations in early 1957. Later in the same year both
committees filed formal reports accusing the NAACP and its attorneys of
engaging in the illegal practice of law. These allegations stemmed from the
committees' findings that integration lawsuits were sponsored by the
NAACP, and that many of the plaintiffs in such suits were unaware that
they were to be the actual litigants. The NAACP lawyers denied that they

solicited clients and maintained that they filed desegregation lawsuits only after being retained as legal counsel. If found guilty of any misconduct, NAACP attorneys faced possible disbarment.[25]

These legislative assaults upon the NAACP were designed to harass, discredit, and cripple the organization in Virginia and thereby to hinder school desegregation. Although eventually dismantled by the courts, the anti-NAACP acts did temporarily stymie NAACP activity by placing it on the defensive and forcing the association to spend considerable time and money protecting itself and trying to regain its legitimacy among blacks. NAACP membership and contributions declined sharply, and by 1957 membership in Virginia had fallen off by about one-third.[26] And though the NAACP suffered only a temporary setback that apparently had no lasting effects, organization leaders realized the destructive potential of such legislation and breathed a sigh of relief once it was declared unconstitutional. Considering the racist and reactionary climate in which the NAACP operated, there was no guarantee that the laws would be overturned, at least without protracted litigation. Oliver W. Hill, chairman of the legal committee of the Virginia NAACP Conference, later commented that the statutes "would have rendered the NAACP impotent in a short while had they not been overturned by the courts."[27]

Against the backdrop of the recently enacted massive–resistance legislation, Virginians prepared for the upcoming gubernatorial election. In November 1957 James Lindsay Almond, who had been attorney general under Governor Stanley, was elected governor of Virginia. After mending political fences with Senator Byrd (who had initially supported state Senator Garland Gray for governor), Almond became a loyal supporter of the Byrd organization and wasted no time expressing his vehement opposition to school desegregation. "We will oppose," Almond's platform read, "with every facility at our command, and with every ounce of our energy, the attempt being made to mix the white and Negro races in our classrooms. Let there be no misunderstanding, no weasel words, on this point: We dedicate our every capacity to preserve segregation in the schools."[28] In less than nine months after his inauguration, Almond would get a chance to prove exactly where he stood.

Understandably, blacks were appalled, but hardly surprised, at Governor Almond's strong statements in support of segregation. Especially troubling to many were the extremes to which Virginia politicians were apparently willing to go in order to preserve segregated schools, which, unfortunately, included the possibility that the schools might be closed just to keep blacks out. Speaking at a mass meeting in Richmond on February 27, 1958, NAACP Executive Secretary Roy Wilkins said: "In Virginia the technique of 'massive resistance' has brought the state to the verge of chaos. The Byrds, the Stanleys, the Almonds, the Grays, and all the lesser lights have spawned confusion worse confounded. Just as the Virginia planners have brought confusion and failure to their own state, so they can claim a large share of the credit . . . for the tension it has aroused in our nation, and for the embarrassment it has brought our country in the world." Oliver Hill, while disgusted over the prospect of school closings, said that if schools had to be closed to "bring Virginia to its senses, then the sooner we reach that crisis the better."[29]

On Friday, September 12, 1958, Warren County High School became the first school in Virginia to be closed under the state's massive–resistance laws. Twenty-two black students had applied for admission, but their applications were rejected and a suit was subsequently filed on August 27, 1958. Under court order to desegregate, the Warren County school superintendent and board of education received the following notice from Governor Almond: "Pursuant to the provisions of Chapter 9.1 of the Code of Virginia, the Warren County High School is closed and is removed from the public school system, effective September 15, 1958, and all authority, power and control over such school, its principal, teachers, other employees and all pupils now enrolled, will thereupon be vested in the Commonwealth of Virginia, to be exercised by the Governor."[30]

Within days the crisis intensified, as the governor closed schools in other localities facing desegregation orders. On September 19 Lane High School and Venable Elementary School in Charlottesville were closed. The next major city affected was Norfolk, Virginia's largest metropolitan area, where six white schools were closed, displacing some 10,000 students.[31]

People throughout the nation were stunned. Virginia's commitment to segregation had never been questioned, and most observers considered Virginia's political leadership to be dead serious about its campaign to prevent integration from taking place. But closing the public schools was no laughing matter, and despite their initial enthusiasm and support for such a bold move, many whites found themselves unprepared to accept the consequences. Parents, politicians, and public–school personnel sought to provide some system of education for the white students who had been displaced by the school closings. Many local buildings were rapidly transformed into makeshift classrooms in order to accommodate the students, and many public-school teachers transferred to private academies, which by now were overflowing. These educational improvisations notwithstanding, several thousand white students in Norfolk received no formal instruction whatsoever through December 1958.[32] Here it was most evident that the various stopgap measures had failed to fill the vacuum created by the absence of public schools. Unfortunately for the students, public schools remained closed throughout the fall in Norfolk, Charlottesville, and Warren County, and there were no indications that Governor Almond was considering altering his position. A showdown was inevitable.

At this point, the courts intervened. On January 19, 1959, the Virginia Supreme Court of Appeals declared in *Harrison v. Day* that the school closings violated section 129 of Virginia's state constitution, which required the state to "maintain an efficient system of public free schools throughout the state." "That means," wrote Chief Justice John W. Eggleston for a five-to-two majority, "that the state must support such public free schools in the state as are necessary to an efficient system, including those in which pupils of both races are compelled to be enrolled and taught together, however unfortunate that situation may be."[33] In a per curiam opinion delivered the same day, a three-judge federal court in Norfolk ruled in *James v. Almond* that Virginia's school-closing statute violated the Fourteenth Amendment, and was therefore null and void. As long as the state maintained a public school system, the court said, "the closing of a public school or grade therein . . . violates the right of a citizen to equal protection of the laws."[34]

Governor Almond seemed undaunted, despite these rulings. Appearing on a television broadcast the next day, he made an emotional last stand in support of segregation:

> To those in high place or elsewhere who advocate integration for your children and send their own to private or public segregated schools; to those who defend or close their eyes to the livid stench of sadism, sex immorality and juvenile pregnancy infesting the mixed schools of the District of Columbia and elsewhere; to those who would overthrow the customs, morals and traditions of a way of life which has endured in honor and decency for centuries and embrace a new moral code prepared by nine men in Washington whose moral concepts they know nothing about; . . . to all of these and their confederates, comrades and allies, let me make it abundantly clear for the record now and hereafter, as governor of this state, I will not yield to that which I know to be wrong and will destroy every semblance of education for thousands of the children of Virginia.[35]

Yet one week later in a surprising about-face, Governor Almond addressed the General Assembly and calmly proposed that Virginia abandon massive resistance. Realizing the futility of continued defiance (and not willing to risk jail for himself), the governor offered no new plans to block school integration in the upcoming school year, and on February 2, 1959, Virginia's era of massive resistance ended abruptly when twenty-one black students entered previously all-white schools in Norfolk and Arlington without incident.[36]

There was, however, one notable exception. Whites in Prince Edward County decided to hold on to massive resistance and eventually chose to abandon public education rather than to submit to a court order to desegregate. In September of 1959 Prince Edward's white children began attending private schools; black parents were advised that their only recourse was to establish private schools for their children. The state offered tuition grants ranging from $125 to $150 to assist white children attending private schools. In addition, citizens of the county received real–estate and personal–property tax credits of up to 25 percent for any contributions made to a nonprofit, nonsectarian private school. No such financial assistance was provided for the county's black children. Except for partial attendance at a few loosely coordinated "training centers," conducted primarily by black college students, most of the county's black children received no more formal education until the Prince Edward Free School Association was established in the fall of 1963.[37]

In August of 1961, the county's black parents filed a suit against the Prince Edward County school board. On July 26, 1962, Federal Judge Oren R. Lewis ordered the school board to submit a plan to reopen the public schools on an integrated basis. No acceptable plan was ever offered, and on May 25, 1964, the United States Supreme Court ordered that a decree be entered that would guarantee public education for black children in Prince Edward. Finally, on June 23, after black students in the county had gone nearly five years without public education, the Prince Edward County Board of Supervisors voted four to two to comply with the federal courts and reopen the public schools on an integrated basis.[38] Massive resistance was dead at last.

The intense emotionalism generated by massive resistance failed to produce a consensus among Virginia's ruling elite as to how prolonged resistance to school desegregation might best be sustained. In fact, a more moderate element had emerged that was beginning to question the efficacy of continued defiance, and it soon became clear that at least some members of Virginia's ruling oligarchy—including such notables as former Governor John S. Battle, University of Virginia President Colgate W. Darden, and Richmond *Times-Dispatch* editor Virginius Dabney—were willing to accept a modicum of integration rather than completely abandon the public–school system. Such a philosophy, however, remained anathema to the die-hard segregationists who were willing to sacrifice public education in order to preserve the remnants of the old plantation social order.[39] Recent court rulings had made it clear that massive resistance was doomed; nonetheless, at least some Virginians believed (or perhaps wanted to believe) that greater solidarity might have made a difference, as is evident in a letter James J. Kilpatrick wrote to Senator Byrd: "United we might have stood for a generation; divided we are falling as surely as a cause can fall."[40]

Historians have long debated Virginia's role in the massive–resistance campaign, and there is a certain ambiguity as to who the real villains were. Benjamin Muse suggests that "Virginia's political leaders, instead of being hog-tied in constructive impulses by the prejudice of their constituents, were actually more extreme in their opposition to school desegregation than the people of the state as a whole."[41] While this is undoubtedly true, J. Harvie Wilkinson III notes that the "people of the state as a whole" were not completely unified in their opposition to school desegregation, and their opinions could vary considerably depending upon which part of the state they lived in. Whites living in Virginia's black belt (where the percentage of blacks was high) were generally more strongly opposed to desegregation than whites living in the northern Virginia suburbs (where the percentage of blacks was low). Yet, in Harry Byrd's Virginia, as Wilkinson observes, "the people of the state as a whole" did not always make the crucial decisions.[42]

Although more calculated than spontaneous, massive resistance, while perhaps not inevitable, was certainly predictable, especially in light of Virginia's political climate in the mid-1950s, the tone of which was determined by Senator Harry Byrd. Wilkinson notes that "more than any other individual, Byrd pushed Virginia into defiance. . . . Byrd coined the phrase 'massive resistance'in February 1956, and . . . he encouraged Lindsay Almond to block integration, and Almond forsook massive resistance only over the adamant objections of Harry Byrd." Almond, in many ways the real tragic figure of the entire episode, later commented: "I lived in hell."[43]

As Virginia's massive resistance lay dying, Richmond's *passive* resistance was just being conceived. Unlike the public–school systems in Norfolk, Charlottesville, and Warren and Prince Edward counties, whose doors were closed in contemptuous defiance of *Brown,* the public schools in Richmond remained open throughout the state's massive resistance cam-paign—open, but segregated. During this time the city learned an invalu-able lesson. Having witnessed the outcome of the state's intense but short-lived resistance, Richmond's public–school officials seemed determined not to repeat that mistake. The state's resistance ultimately crumbled because of its insistence upon becoming embroiled in constitutional warfare with the Supreme Court, clearly a foolhardy venture. Richmond's officials, on the other hand, while equally committed to maintaining segregated schools, were considerably less conspicuous in the pursuit of their objectives. If they could convince the courts that they were acting in good faith by admitting a few "token" black students to formerly all–white schools, then school integration in Richmond might possibly be forestalled for yet another generation. And so it was.

School board chairman Lewis F. Powell, Jr., promised in 1959 that "public education will be continued in our city—although every proper effort will be made to minimize the extent of integration when it comes." Powell realized that some integration was inevitable, and said that Richmond had to choose "between some integration or the abandonment of our public school education." But in an attempt to allay the fears of the rabid segregationists, he issued an ominous prediction: "We foresee no substantial integration in the elementary schools of Richmond. This is true because there are sufficient elementary schools . . . to serve adequately both races. . . . There are, indeed, sound reasons to believe that a majority of the elementary schools will have no more than [a] negligible percentage of integration for many years."[44] Although Powell had predicted continued segregation only in the city's elementary schools, "separate but equal" remained firmly intact in the middle and high schools as well. By 1959, fewer than 1 percent of Virginia's black students attended desegregated schools, and no desegregation whatsoever had occurred in Virginia's capital city.

Richmond in 1956 was a thoroughly segregated city and a perfect illustration of what "separate but equal" was in reality. In no area of public policy was racial separation more pronounced than in the city's housing patterns. In his study of twentieth–century Richmond, Christopher Silver notes that housing in the core city became increasingly racially segregated after 1900.[45] Municipal ordinances, which restricted blacks to specific areas, were effective means of promoting race separation, and when they were outlawed by the United States Supreme Court in 1917, restrictive covenants took their place.[46] Because Richmond had a sizeable black community, Silver writes, the city's white residents regarded racially conscious planning as "a necessary vehicle to ensure race separation and black political impotence within a dynamic metropolis."[47] And because of their preoccupation with suburban expansion and development in white residential areas, Richmond's planners neglected the mounting problems facing black core-city residents. This neglect eventually resulted in urban decay and substandard housing conditions that prompted a growing number of whites to abandon the inner city and to seek a better life in the suburbs.[48]

By the early 1950s, residential segregation had become firmly established in Richmond. Richmond's white businessmen utilized numerous devices to maintain segregation in many areas. Real estate brokers would not show black families houses in white neighborhoods, nor would they show white families houses in black neighborhoods. Bankers refused to lend money to a black family that was considering buying a home in a white residential area. The Federal Housing Administration would not insure home loans in those areas that were not racially homogeneous. In this manner, local businessmen were able to perpetuate de facto segregation until Congress passed the Fair Housing Act in 1968.[49]

On the other hand, as some blacks, emboldened by the Supreme Court's 1948 ruling in *Shelley v. Kraemer,* began to move into previously all–white neighborhoods, whites gradually moved out until the entire neighborhood soon became overwhelmingly black. For instance, Richmond's Church Hill, practically all-white in 1950, had become predominantly black by the late 1960s. This pattern of migration, known as the policy of conversion, was commonplace in Richmond during this period and soon gained acceptance as a popular escape valve for whites once all legal barriers to integrated housing had fallen.[50]

The consequences of Richmond's history of inadequate and segregated housing for blacks were profound. The educational instruction provided for black schoolchildren living in impoverished neighborhoods followed the discriminatory pattern evident in the city's housing policy. Firmly established residential segregation would seriously hamper future attempts to desegregate the unequal public schools.

Richmond's public–school system in the early 1950s was a classic example of the contradictions inherent in "separate but equal." Measured in terms of the quality and size of buildings, availability of facilities, and teachers' salaries, black schools lagged far behind. Owing to insufficient funds and a lack of concern on the part of the white community, all of the black schools were structurally inferior to the white schools and lacked many of the facilities—such as science labs, auditoriums, and athletic fields—that were common at white schools. Many of the educational supplies provided to the black schools, such as desks, maps, and books, were those that had been discarded by white schools. Not surprisingly, these supplies were usually outdated and in very poor condition. George L. Jones, a current administrator in the Richmond Public School System, remembers what it was like in the 1950s: "When I was a student at Armstrong [all-black] many of the books that we used came from Thomas Jefferson [all-white], and no attempt was made to conceal the fact that we were getting hand-me-down books because the 'Thomas Jefferson' stamp was still in the books. The first Latin book I ever used was one that had been thrown out by Thomas Jefferson, with several pages torn out. That kind of thing was quite common."[51]

The problems confronting black teachers in Richmond's segregated school system were immense, and the enormous disparities and inadequacies that existed made it impossible for black children to receive an education comparable to that whites received. Most black teachers agreed that the greatest problem facing them under the dual school system was the shortage of classroom space. According to Nathaniel Lee, a music teacher at all-black Maggie Walker High School, overcrowding was so bad that "one school [all-black Woodville Elementary] had twenty-six classes on double shift, so that kids were in school half a day; some went in the morning, and some went in the afternoon—and this lasted until about 1965."[52]

One of the most blatant trademarks of the separate–but–equal system was the enormous disparity in teachers' salaries. During the 1940s, the annual salaries for Richmond's black teachers ranged from a minimum of

$300 to a maximum of $900; for whites, the beginning salary was $1,000 and could go as high as $1,900. In addition to the monetary discrepancies, black teachers were much less secure in their positions than whites because the absence of a tenure system meant that any teacher could be dismissed arbitrarily, without justification. Consequently, most blacks passively accepted racial pay differentials out of fear of losing their jobs. Indeed, many black teachers had their contracts terminated after agreeing to serve as plaintiffs in a discrimination suit.[53]

It was the unequal pay scale that first prompted the NAACP to launch an all-out campaign against racial discrimination in education. *Plessy v. Ferguson,* the 1896 Supreme Court case that sanctioned separate but equal, was still the law of the land. Up until the early 1950s, NAACP strategy had been to oppose discrimination within the existing framework of separate but equal, believing that it would be risky to challenge segregation.[54] Because of the disparities that existed between black and white schools, it was generally not a difficult task for NAACP lawyers to prove that facilities for blacks were both inadequate and inferior. The NAACP contended that if *Plessy* were to be the guiding principle, then "equal" would have to be enforced as rigorously as "separate." By demanding equal facilities, the NAACP hoped to make the cost of operating a dual school system so expensive that economic considerations alone would force white Southerners to abandon segregation.[55] But it soon became clear that whites were willing to pay almost any price to preserve their racial caste system.[56]

An increasing number of black psychologists and sociologists, Kenneth B. Clark the best-known among them, began to cite the adverse psychological effects that segregation had on black children. These social scientists, along with attorneys for the NAACP, argued that new buses and brick buildings could not compensate for the humiliation, the lack of dignity and self-respect, that blacks suffered as a result of being segregated from white children. W. Lester Banks, Virginia's NAACP executive secretary, remarked that a newly constructed black school could not be equal to a new white school "if it were built brick for brick, cement for cement."[57] In short, NAACP leaders were more convinced than ever before that separate but equal was a cruel hoax and that black children would never receive an equal education as long as they were separated from white children. They hoped that the present Vinson Court would be more sympathetic to that argument than the 1896 Court had been.

None of the NAACP's leaders was more dedicated to the struggle for social justice than Richmond attorney Oliver W. Hill. One of the unsung heroes of the early civil rights struggle, Hill served as chairman of the Virginia NAACP legal staff. The fact that he has remained relatively obscure for so long testifies to the quiet and unassuming manner in which he performed his duties. Hill's first involvement in racial discrimination litigation came in 1941, when he and associate Samuel W. Tucker filed a suit against the city of Richmond to equalize teacher salaries. Hill's law practice was briefly interrupted in 1943 when he was drafted into the U.S. army. After completing service in World War II, Hill returned to Richmond to set up a law practice and to continue his work with the NAACP. Later, Hill, along with Robert Carter and Spottswood Robinson, served as legal counsel for the plaintiffs in Prince Edward's school desegregation case. In a 1985 interview, Hill explained why the NAACP made the bold decision to scrap equalization suits and pursue complete desegregation:

> We never felt that the segregation laws were constitutional, but we also felt that to try to go from complete segregation to complete integration in one fell swoop would probably be too much, and we knew that we needed to educate the courts and the public. Our initial approach was to tackle the problem of inferior facilities at Negro schools, and to try to force whites to make the schools equal; we felt that if we did that, then maybe they would get sense enough to recognize the fact that it would be simpler and cheaper to operate one school than two—but it didn't work out that way. We found out that all we were doing was getting little–better segregated schools, and in some instances they weren't better; sometimes they were new, but they were never equal. For example, once we started pushing them real strong, that's when they came in with the combination of the cafeteria-auditorium-library, all in one, just to say that they were doing something when in fact they were doing very little. We realized that to push for total desegregation would be risky, and that "Jim Crow" would be more deeply entrenched than ever if we lost, but it was a gamble we had to take.[58]

Despite a barrage of antisegregation lawsuits filed by the NAACP, Richmond's officials demonstrated no willingness whatsoever to modify existing segregation laws or to make any concessions to the city's black residents, although blacks made up a third of the city's population. That white Richmonders had no intentions of sharing power with blacks became evident when the city's black residents appealed to the city council for representation on the school board. On August 7, 1950, Richmond's only black newspaper, the *Afro-American,* formally petitioned Mayor T. Nelson Parker and the members of the city council to appoint a black to the school board to fill the unexpired term of Guy B. Hazelgrove, a Richmond attorney who had died on August 3. The *Afro-American* recommended Oliver W. Hill, attorney and former councilman, for "serious consideration."[59] Mayor Parker replied to the letter on August 9, stating that the *Afro-American*'s request would be presented to the city council for consideration and that its recommendation would have "the thoughtful consideration of myself and all other members of the city council." The *Afro-American*'s letter emphasized two points: first, that although the city's black residents had the greatest respect for most of the white school board members, the fact remained that there were still no blacks serving on the board; and second, that choosing Oliver Hill to fill the vacancy would not only give the city's blacks some long-overdue representation on the school board but would also bring to the board an experienced attorney who had devoted much of his life to the fight against racial injustice.[60]

When the nine-member council met the following week, it ignored the pleas of the black Richmonders and voted seven to nothing (with two members abstaining) to appoint Lewis F. Powell, a white Richmond attorney, to fill the vacancy. Powell, a member of the prestigious law firm of Hunton, Williams, Anderson, Gay & Moore, and destined to become an associate justice on the United States Supreme Court, became chairman of Richmond's school board in 1952 and held that position until 1961. Despite this setback, Richmond blacks continued to put pressure on the city council to appoint a black to the school board, and in 1953 prominent businessman Booker T. Bradshaw became the first black since Reconstruction to be named to Richmond's school board. He was appointed vice-chairman in 1960 and remained a member of the board until 1965.[61]

The NAACP had forced the South to improve the facilities at many of the black schools, but there were no indications that the segregationists were ready to open white schools to black children. In fact, one of the greatest ironies of the NAACP's equalization victories was that by eliminating the physical inequities associated with the dual system of education, the NAACP had corrected the most palpable defect, thereby unwittingly discrediting its own argument that separate could never be equal. As a result, segregation appeared to some to be more deeply entrenched than ever.

Civil rights attorneys continued to file desegregation suits in the nation's highest court, and the justices, while continuing to uphold *Plessy*, were growing increasingly sympathetic to the black plaintiffs as it became more apparent that most white state officials were serious only about providing black children with a separate education, not an equal one. State and local officials began to sense that judicial support for separate but equal was waning, and it seemed to them that the Court was moving closer to desegregation all the time. Fearing that a desegregation order was imminent and hoping to forestall what they considered judicial madness, white school officials all across the South made desperate attempts to improve all black schools. Virginia was no exception.

In August 1953, Virginia's state board of education presented an all-time high budget proposal to the commissioners, aimed at achieving parity in all of Virginia's public schools by the 1954–55 school year. The state requested an unprecedented $40,807,500 for the purpose of filling teacher vacancies, building construction, improvements, and operating expenses in white and black schools. Richmond's schools, especially its black schools, were targeted to receive a large share of the funds. The board requested an additional $18,800 for recently renovated Armstrong, which would be used for an electric panel and eight tables for the physics laboratory, eight workbenches for the chemistry laboratory, and a drill press for the machine shop. In addition, $18,000 would be appropriated to repair the stage at Cardozo, $6,500 would be spent to renovate the school rifle range, $2,500 would be allocated to replace the rest room and dressing-room equipment at Dunbar Elementary, and more than $20,000 would be earmarked for improvements at Eliot Junior High School, to include furniture for two art rooms, a metal shop, furniture and equipment for three science rooms, and typewriter tables and chairs. Similar improvements at Dunbar were estimated at $21,900.[62]

As it turned out, these efforts by state and local officials proved to be in vain. Little did they know that within less than a year the Warren-led Supreme Court would earn its place in history by drastically altering the course of race relations in the United States. The country was poised on the threshold of a social revolution. But, on the battlefield where it would take place, the revolution would still be fiercely resisted for a generation.

The *Brown* decision brought about no immediate changes in the way Richmond's public schools operated. In fact, city officials seemed to ignore the Court's ruling altogether, taking comfort instead in segregationist pronouncements that the actual implementation of such a far-reaching decision was many years away. City officials in Richmond, like those in other localities throughout the state, were in a quandary as to how they should deal with the problems posed by the *Brown* decision, as the state's massive resistance was at high tide. Therefore, on June 9, 1955, Richmond's school board announced that it would be "premature for the Richmond School Board to take any action on this subject [school desegregation] until such time as it is known what policy will be established on the State level."[63]

Anticipating that some school boards might not voluntarily accept massive resistance, Virginia's General Assembly enacted legislation that withdrew from local boards the authority to assign pupils in a way that would achieve desegregation. This authority would now be vested in the newly created Pupil Placement Board. Once the state announced its new pupil assignment policy, Richmond's school board seemed willing to comply. This legislative maneuver enabled the state and the city to work together for the next ten years to deny black children the rights that had been granted to them by the United States Supreme Court.

The highest court in the land had ruled that separation of the races in the public schools was unconstitutional; yet, Richmond's public schools continued to operate under the dual school system. One court decision could not eradicate the shameful legacy of separate but equal, and the prevailing assumption among both blacks and whites alike was that resistance to school integration would not disappear, but would merely present itself in a more sophisticated guise. And when one considers the sincerity of white Southern devotion to the maintenance of a racial caste system, it becomes apparent that any other course of action would have been antithetical to Southern custom. If Virginia's early surrender had demonstrated the futility of open defiance, then Richmond's prolonged resistance would demonstrate the efficacy of more subtle delaying tactics and evasive maneuvers when implemented under the pretense of gradual compliance. By late 1956, the transformation had begun.

TWO

The Policy of Containment, 1956–65

This newspaper has concluded, in the light of recent events, that new defenses are urgently needed. If Virginia is to avoid defeat—if we are to be spared the awful tragedy of violence and race hatred that would result from integrated public schools to which there was no workable alterna- tive—then we must prepare ourselves for speedy abandonment of a legal position that cannot be held much longer.

—Richmond *News Leader,* 1958

We must now reconsider and realign our echelons of defense [against the Supreme Court's desegregation decision]. We have been fighting, in effect, on the enemy's own terms, under conditions and restrictions most favorable to him and unfavorable to us. This is suicidal. We must now find another position from which to fight, with ground for maneuver, to gather our strength and renew the battle.

—Richmond *Times-Dispatch,* 1958

Created in response to the *Brown* decision, Virginia's Pupil Placement Board officially came into existence on December 29, 1956. Touted by the Richmond newspapers as Virginia's "first line of defense against integra- tion," the three-member Pupil Placement Board was empowered by the General Assembly to assume all responsibilities for pupil assignments and school transfers throughout the state. These powers had formerly rested with local school boards. Under the new statute, students would automati- cally return to the schools they were attending at the time the law became effective. As a result, many Virginia localities, including Richmond, continued to operate segregated schools, because no desegregation had occurred before December 29, 1956. In theory, the board was authorized to perpetuate segregation by assigning pupils to specific schools for any of a variety of reasons except race or color. In actuality, race was the sole criterion considered; the Pupil Placement Board assigned very few black students to white schools in Virginia while it remained in operation. In many instances, these assignments resulted from a direct court order. During its years of operation, the Pupil Placement Board relied on residential housing patterns and lower academic achievement to disqualify blacks from being eligible to enroll in white schools.[1]

The state's new pupil–assignment policy began with the distribution of 75,000 "Applications for Placement of Pupil" forms. The forms, printed in triplicate, were sent to parents or guardians of children who were: (1) entering school in Virginia for the first time; (2) being graduated from one school to another within the same school division; (3) transferring to another school division; or (4) entering a public school after the beginning of the session. Although there was no place on the form for stating the child's race, a birth certificate (on which race was indicated) or a photostatic copy of it was required for any student who had moved to Virginia from another state and sought to enroll in Virginia schools for the first time. On the back of the form was a space for the local school board to make any "comments concerning pupil" and to make recommendations regarding the school to which the pupil should be assigned.[2]

On December 26, 1956, Governor Stanley appointed a school superintendent, a lawyer, and a newspaper executive as the first three members of the Pupil Placement Board. Hugh V. White, Nansemond County Superintendent of Schools; Beverly H. Randolph, Jr., a Richmond attorney who lived in Charles City County; and Andrew A. Farley, vice-president and general manager of the Register Publishing Company of Danville all resided in areas with large black populations. Blacks made up 65 percent of the population in Nansemond County, 81 percent in Charles City County, and 30 percent in Danville. Not surprisingly, all three were strongly opposed to mixed public schools. In this regard, they were eminently qualified for the positions they were about to fill. The day after their appointment the Richmond *Times-Dispatch* hailed the Pupil Placement Board as "a crucially important instrument in opposition to public school integration," and praised the appointees as dedicated citizens who were "well-qualified for the duties entrusted to them."[3]

On August 5, 1957, the newly appointed board members issued a statement that set forth their position very clearly. Contained in the statement were two provisions that best summarized the purpose and intent of the Pupil Placement Board:

1. No child can be legally enrolled in the public schools of the Commonwealth of Virginia until an application has been filed in his behalf, unless he remains in the school in which he was enrolled prior to December 29, 1956.
2. In the event there is a refusal on the part of the parent or legal guardian of the pupil to file an application in the pupil's behalf, at that moment the pupil is

no longer legally enrolled, and should not be allowed to further attend the public schools of Virginia.[4]

Within weeks after the Pupil Placement Board outlined its objectives, the Parent-Teachers Association from black Baker Elementary School in Richmond circulated flyers urging black parents not to sign the pupil placement forms. The Richmond *Afro-American* also implored the black community not to comply with this law. By early June, parents of more than three hundred black children had refused to sign the forms. Oliver Hill, legal counsel for the parents, issued a statement denouncing the Pupil Placement Board as blatantly discriminatory and a clear violation of *Brown*. Hill said that the Pupil Placement Act had been "clearly and unequivocally designed to maintain segregation in Virginia. . . . Not a single Negro child has been placed in a white school." The names of all parents who refused to sign the forms were reported to the board and to Richmond School Superintendent Henry I. Willett. It was agreed that no action would be taken during the 1956–57 school year and that the students would be allowed to complete the term without disruption, despite their parents' refusal to comply with state law.[5]

When schools opened in Richmond for the 1957–58 school year, approximately 150 black children showed up without the Pupil Placement Board application forms. Roughly one hundred of them were sent home, while the others, for various reasons, were allowed to remain in school for a fifteen-day grace period. A few days later a group of black parents, led by Alice R. Calloway, decided to challenge the constitutionality of the Pupil Placement Board in the federal courts. Oliver Hill would represent them.[6]

In the meantime, several "child care units" were organized for black children who had been displaced as a result of the pupil–assignment controversy. Chester M. Hampton, president of the newly organized Richmond Pupil Protective Association, commented that these care centers "won't be schools, but they will be places where the children will be under supervision. . . . We also expect, from the statements of our members, that parents will welcome having some place to keep their older children off the streets." Parents, teachers, and a number of postal employees volunteered their services as full– or part–time supervisors at the centers. More than ten churches throughout the city offered their facilities to help accommodate the one hundred or so displaced students.[7]

The children stayed out of city schools for nearly two weeks before Oliver Hill was able to get Judge Sterling Hutcheson to grant an order temporarily restraining the enforcement of the pupil–placement plan in Richmond. The order, issued on September 17, 1957, meant that children of parents, white or black, who refused to sign the forms could not be denied admission to city schools, and that all such children who had been expelled had to be readmitted immediately. Judge Hutcheson maintained that his chief concern was for the welfare of the children, who he felt would suffer unnecessarily if they could not attend school. "I feel that under the circumstances that the children involved here are the ones primarily affected," the judge said. A. B. Scott, attorney for the placement board, argued that such an order was in direct violation of state law. "There is nothing in the world to prevent these children from entering schools if they comply with the law," Scott declared. He accused the defiant parents of "flaunting" state laws. Meanwhile, the Pupil Placement Board estimated that throughout the state about five–thousand placement forms had been signed "under protest." The children involved were permitted to remain in school, and the temporary restraining order remained in effect for the rest of the school year.[8]

The first major challenge in Richmond to the pupil assignment plan began in the summer of 1958. Before that time, black parents had merely criticized the assignment plan in principle; none had directly challenged it by trying to enroll their children in white schools. In July, six black children applied for admission to all-white Nathaniel Bacon and West-hampton elementary schools. The six applicants, Onslow Minnis, Sylvester Smith, Jerome Smith, Daisy Jane Cooper, Wanda Irene Dabney, and Lorna Renee Warden, ranged in age from five to nine; all lived closer to the white schools they were applying to than they did to the black schools they were then attending. Acting on the advice of the city attorney, Richmond's school board promptly announced that it had no authority under state law to assign children to public schools and that the applications would be referred to the state Pupil Placement Board. No one seriously expected the Pupil Placement Board to assign any of the black children to a white school, since the board was part of the machinery that Virginia had created to perpetuate segregation. Further, the enrollment of a single black student in a white public school would automatically bring about the closing of that school under Virginia's anti-integration laws. As expected, on August 29 all six applications were denied.[9]

The parents of the six black children filed suit in the United States District Court on September 2, 1958.[10] Martin A. Martin, attorney for the plaintiffs, argued that each of the six black children had made "timely" application to attend Richmond's white schools during the 1958–59 session, but were denied solely on account of their race. He also emphasized that although only six plaintiffs were named, the suit was being filed on behalf of all black children in Richmond similarly situated. Martin asked for a hearing the following Monday, as that was the day that the city's schools were scheduled to open for the 1958–59 school year. The case would not be settled until nearly three years later.[11]

Meanwhile, on February 24, 1960, all three members of the Pupil Placement Board announced their intention to resign, effective June 1. All

three—Andrew A. Farley, Hugh V. White, and Beverly H. Randolph, Jr.—
had served on the board since first being appointed to the newly formed
board by Governor Stanley in December 1956. Each of them cited personal
reasons for resigning, but in fact their resignations were in protest against
the state's new local option pupil–assignment plan, scheduled to go into
effect March 1, 1960. Under the new law, the state Pupil Placement Board
would continue to have statewide authority in the matter of pupil assignments, but a locality could now opt to remove itself from under the placement board's jurisdiction. This could only be done, however, if both the
local school board and the local governing body agreed. In their closing
report, the placement board members said that their policy had been "to
fight, with every legal and honorable means, any attempted mixing of the
races in the public schools." They added: "The board does not feel that it
was, nor should its successors feel that they should be, obligated to take one
positive step toward the mixing of the races in the public schools."[12]

While the *Warden* case was still pending, Governor Almond appointed
three new members to the Pupil Placement Board. Earnest J. Oglesby was
a math professor at the University of Virginia and president of the
Albemarle–Charlottesville chapter of the segregationist Defenders of State
Sovereignty and Individual Liberties; Alfred L. Wingo was coordinator of
testing, guidance, and research in the State Department of Education; and
Edward T. Justis was assistant supervisor of rehabilitation in the State
Department of Education. At their first meeting on August 15, 1960, the
new appointees considered the applications of four black children who had
applied for transfer to white schools in Richmond. They rejected two on
the grounds that they lived closer to a black school; but, in a move that
broke with the board's past practice, they approved the transfer of the two
who lived closer to a white school.[13] This was the first time that the Pupil
Placement Board had voluntarily assigned black children to white schools
in Richmond. When Gloria Jean Mead, age thirteen, and Carol Irene
Swann, age twelve, quietly entered the eighth grade at Chandler Junior
High School on September 6, 1960, the first crack in Richmond's armor of
school segregation had been made.[14]

Despite the admission of two blacks to Chandler, Richmond's armor of
segregation proved to be extremely durable, however, and would continue
to ward off the attacks on segregation for years to come. Technically,
school desegregation in Richmond had finally begun, but the slow pace at
which it proceeded dramatically reduced its significance. This policy of
containment—or tokenism—had been designed to keep school desegregation to a minimum. It was the next best thing to massive resistance. And it
worked: by September 1960, out of nearly 204,000 black pupils throughout
the entire state, fewer than 170 in eleven Virginia localities were enrolled in
white schools.[15]

Wallace Reid Calloway, a twelve–year–old black student at Graves
Junior High School, was among those denied admission to Chandler.
Wallace's father, William C. Calloway, Sr., was a prominent black physician in the city. His mother, Alice Calloway, was a well–respected civic
leader who had served as chairperson of the committee responsible for
arranging child care units during the fall of 1957, when a number of black
children, including her own, had been expelled from city schools because of
their parents' refusal to sign the pupil–placement forms. Alice Calloway
had a well–deserved reputation for being a conscientious, civic–minded individual who possessed exceptional leadership qualities and was unafraid to
challenge any system that denied her her constitutional rights.

Segregation was nothing new to Alice Calloway. Born in Portsmouth,
Virginia, and reared in Richmond, she knew well enough what it was like to
be black in a thoroughly segregated city. She remembers one particular
incident that occurred in Bryan Park in Richmond in the summer of 1956
that still serves as a painful reminder of the daily indignities once heaped
upon blacks in the name of white supremacy. She and some friends were
trying to have a picnic in the park when the park superintendent approached
them and demanded to know what they were doing there. The group of
blacks replied that they were having a picnic. The park superintendent then
informed them that the park was reserved for whites only. The blacks, led
by Alice Calloway, refused to leave. Miffed, the park superintendent made
a list of all of the names of the "agitators," accused them of having been
sent by the NAACP to stir up trouble, and then sent for the director of parks
and recreation. At this point, Alice Calloway called Oliver Hill, who
instructed her not to be intimidated, because she and her friends had every
right to use park facilities. Shortly thereafter the director arrived on the
scene and immediately summoned the police, who arrived in several squad
cars a few moments later. The chief of police approached the blacks and
ordered them to leave. Still they refused. When he realized that the blacks
were not going to leave the park and were obviously willing to go to jail for
their civil disobedience, the chief of police retreated and decided not to
make a scene. Alice Calloway and her friends were then left alone to enjoy
their picnic.[16]

Alice Calloway has spoken of the Bryan Park incident on many
occasions, each time with renewed interest and enthusiasm. Always
graceful and modest in her quiet, dignified manner, she nonetheless exudes
a strong sense of pride and personal satisfaction when she recalls that her
show of defiance represented a major victory not only for blacks in
Richmond but for oppressed peoples everywhere. But winning one battle
does not always win the war, and for Alice Calloway and other blacks in
Richmond, the struggle to desegregate the public schools was just beginning.

On September 12 the placement board held a hearing on the matter concerning Wallace Reid Calloway. The board stated that its decision to deny admission to Calloway rested on the fact that he lived closer to Graves than to Chandler. William C. Calloway, Sr., maintained that the shortest distance from his home was 1.9 miles to Graves, and 1.6 miles to Chandler. He further stated that his son had to walk eight-tenths of a mile to catch the bus for Graves, compared to only a block for a bus to Chandler. But the school board presented figures from the city traffic engineer that contradicted Calloway's claim. These figures showed the distance from the Calloway home to be 1.54 miles to Graves and 1.69 miles to Chandler. Oliver Hill, Calloway's attorney, contended that the distance should have been measured from the home to the schools, and not the nearest intersections. The board agreed to have new measurements taken that, it was hoped, would resolve the dispute once and for all.[17]

A few days later, the placement board hired a consulting engineering firm to measure the distance from the Calloway home to each of the schools. Using a surveyor's chain, two engineers, on their hands and knees, measured the distance foot by foot from the home to each of the schools and then, as a double check, from the schools to the home. The measurements showed that the Calloways lived 8,150 feet from Graves, and 8,530 feet from Chandler. On September 26, the placement board reaffirmed its previous decision denying Wallace Reid Calloway admission to Chandler. Alice Calloway later remarked, "I would never have believed that city and state officials would go to such lengths to keep blacks out of white schools."[18]

The Calloway case clearly exemplifies the extent to which residence was often a factor in determining which schools black and white pupils would attend. As noted earlier, a history of segregated housing patterns in Richmond had kept blacks confined to certain areas. Consequently, black schools had been built in black neighborhoods. Therefore, when blacks applied to white schools, they were often told that their interests could best be served by attending the schools in their own neighborhoods and thus were refused admission. Though residential segregation certainly facilitated the school board's racist zoning policy, it was not a prerequisite for school segregation, as black and white children living in the *same* neighborhood were often assigned to different schools.[19]

Well aware of the extent of residential segregation, white moderates began to suggest that further blatant defiance of *Brown* might be unnecessary, as most of them were convinced that token integration schemes would satisfy the courts. In many cases, demographic factors and residential patterns meant that only a small amount of desegregation would occur. As early as 1955, the Richmond *News Leader* predicted that segregated public schools would exist in Richmond "for many years to come, whether in defiance of the Supreme Court's opinion or in acceptance of it." The reason for this was that "school districts will be drawn by white and colored neighborhoods, and where segregation cannot be accomplished by districting, it will be achieved by individual pupil transfers and voluntary choice of schools."[20] Interestingly enough, the Richmond *News Leader* perceived pupil transfers and freedom of choice, not as ways of achieving integration, but as methods of perpetuating segregation.

Most Virginia moderates came from the mountain counties of southwest Virginia or from the Shenandoah Valley, where blacks constituted less than 10 percent of the population. Some hailed from predominantly white suburbs near Arlington and Fairfax. The fact that whites in these areas came into less contact with blacks tended to temper their enthusiasm for uncompromising defiance. In fact, some of these whites indicated that they might even welcome limited integration, as it would relieve them of the costly expense of providing a separate education for a handful of black students. They believed that local–option plans would make it possible for school districts to comply with *Brown* and still preserve the essentials of the dual school system.[21]

State Senator Ted Dalton, a leading moderate from Radford (which had a black population of 5 percent), explained in 1959 that "the schools can be kept 99 percent segregated under local assignment plans" if pupil placement boards assigned students on the basis of scholastic aptitude, geographic location, and enrollment capacity. Such sentiments were echoed by state Senator Armistead Boothe, a leading moderate from the northern Virginia suburbs, who argued that desegregation did "not mean that a predominantly white school will have a large number of Negro pupils or that a predominantly Negro school will have a large number of white pupils." Similarly, school officials in Richmond assured parents that very little integration would occur as long as students were assigned to the schools in their own neighborhoods. "For the past several years," they explained, "schools have been built in neighborhoods in which one race predominates, rather than near the border between a white and Negro residential area. Thus . . . many schools would continue the way they are now."[22]

Although most moderates believed that the essence of segregation could be maintained through local assignment plans (which practically guaranteed that desegregation would be kept to a minimum), the consensus among most of the resisters was that even the slightest retreat from massive resistance would ultimately result in full-scale integration. Senator Byrd declared that "it is either massive resistance or in the long run massive integration, and this would destroy our entire school system." Lindsay Almond was convinced that he knew of "no degree of integration, except as it would be measured by the NAACP—and with them it's total integration."

In a speech delivered in Portsmouth, Virginia, in 1959 Roy Wilkins made it clear that the NAACP would not be satisfied as long as the majority of blacks was enrolled in predominantly black schools. "Negro citizens cannot accept token integration as a satisfaction of the Supreme Court ruling," Wilkins said. "They can accept it only as a beginning, not as an end."[23]

Although it would not become an explosive issue until a decade later, some Virginians were already predicting that busing would eventually be used as a desegregation tool. The Richmond *Times-Dispatch* warned on March 26, 1957: "the NAACP is not content with such integration as would take place along neighborhood lines. They wish to uproot white children from white schools, and uproot colored children from colored schools, in order to expedite race-mingling-by-force." A year later, Lindsay Almond predicted: "we may expect a judicial order to transport Negro children to schools in white areas with the return trip loaded with white children to be forced into Negro schools."[24] Senator Byrd expressed grave concern about the social intimacy that would no doubt accompany any massive integration plan. "The classroom is only one part of it," he cautioned. "School integration means that the white and black children, beginning at the age of 6, will be packed together in the same buses, and all school activities, such as dances, football, basketball, etc., will have to be mixed."[25]

The opponents of school integration believed that the implications of *Brown* would extend far beyond the classroom and into the realm of social interaction, which would ultimately pose a grave threat to the sanctity of the white race. Although racial prejudice was a key factor in the equation, the South's opposition to school integration cannot be totally explained within such a narrow scope. At stake here was a way of life. Whites feared that if blacks could demonstrate that they could excel in any field of endeavor if given opportunities equal to those whites received, then they would prove once and for all that their exclusion from white society was based, not on their innate racial inferiority, but on whites' ingrained racial prejudice. Hence, the notion of racial inferiority would be exposed as a vicious lie, and segregation could no longer be justified.

Although massive resistance was dead, Richmond's local officials were not yet ready to accept school integration as a fait accompli, and their reluctance to move beyond their policy of containment bears testimony to the sincerity of their convictions. Yet, despite their disdain for integration, most officials remained committed to the preservation of public education. Lewis F. Powell, Jr., chairman of the school board from 1952 to 1961, rejected outright the suggestion that Richmond abandon public education in favor of private schools. He believed that while private schools might work in certain localities, "the inescapable truth is that this is not feasible for

Richmond." Powell noted that the existing private schools were already
overcrowded, "and the children so served will largely come from the upper
income brackets, leaving the great masses of middle and lower income
families of both races still dependent entirely on free public education."
For Powell and many others, the question was no longer "if" desegregation,
but "how much?"[26]

One of the most effective ways of minimizing desegregation was the
policy of conversion. When black migration began to threaten the racial
homogeneity of an all-white residential area, whites began to move elsewhere. Consequently, the schools that had formerly served white students
were suddenly "converted" to black schools and clearly designated as such.
The following case, which involved the conversion of *white* Franklin
Elementary to *black* Franklin Elementary, is typical. Notice that the school
board resolution makes no reference to race:

> In light of the crowded conditions at Blackwell Elementary School [black] and
> available facilities at Westover Hills Elementary School and Patrick Henry
> Elementary School [both white], the School Board requests that the Pupil
> Placement Board approve in principle the assignment of certain elementary
> pupils from Blackwell Elementary School to Franklin Elementary School and
> the assignment of certain pupils from Franklin Elementary School to Westover
> Hills Elementary School and Patrick Henry Elementary School. It is under-
> stood that the names of all such pupils will have to be presented to the Pupil
> Placement Board and acted upon in accordance with their normal procedure.[27]

School board members insisted that these conversions were made for the
benefit of the city's black community, so as to relieve overcrowding in
some of the schools. But occasionally their unguarded statements revealed
their ulterior motive. For instance, when considering the feasibility of
converting Chandler Junior High School from white to black, board
members acknowledged that "a majority of the Board believes that conversion of Chandler should minimize the integration problem which confronts
Richmond—although the plan to convert was based entirely on unrelated
considerations." More often than not, those "unrelated considerations"
alluded to by board members were never disclosed.[28]

The policy of conversion clearly shows that not only did the school
board have some control over school desegregation, but that the underlying
intent of both the school board and the Pupil Placement Board was one and
the same—to preserve segregated schools. Although the Pupil Placement
Board technically had control over pupil assignment, approximately 98
percent of the placements were made in accordance with attendance zones
previously designed by the school board. Because the school board had
drawn the zones to perpetuate segregation, the Pupil Placement Board had
no inclination to alter those zones. Nine years after *Brown,* the directory of
the Richmond Public Schools, compiled by the school board, listed "White

Schools" in one division and "Negro Schools" in the other. Thus it was apparent that Richmond had dual school–attendance areas and that assignments were made pursuant to the dual attendance lines.[29]

In July 1961 a series of events began that would eventually bring about the demise of tokenism. The Pupil Placement Board was coming under increasing pressure from the courts to assign more blacks to white schools. During the 1961–62 school year, white Richmond schools admitted twenty-nine blacks while denying admission to twenty others. Local civil rights attorneys were becoming increasingly frustrated with the school board's delaying tactics and, along with the NAACP, continued to demand speedier compliance with *Brown*. Such was the state of affairs in Richmond when the first *Bradley* case reached the courts.

In 1961, in *Bradley v. Richmond School Board*, eleven black parents brought a class-action suit against the Richmond School Board to desegregate the public schools. The plaintiffs' attorneys argued that during the 1961–62 school year the Pupil Placement Board assigned pupils to Richmond schools on the basis of dual attendance zones; that promotions were controlled by a "feeder" system in which black pupils were promoted routinely only to black schools; and that, in the handling of transfer requests from black students, school authorities subjected the applicants to criteria from which white students of the same scholastic aptitude were exempt. The attorneys further maintained that some black applicants, who had been denied admission to white schools on the grounds that they lived closer to a black school, actually lived in overlapping attendance zones, so that while they may have lived closer to a black school, had they been white, they would have been routinely assigned to white schools. Indeed, white students who lived next door to black applicants were assigned to white schools, while the blacks were rejected.

The district court agreed, and, on July 26, 1962, ordered that the eleven pupils be admitted to the white schools.[30] Viewing this as a shallow victory, the plaintiffs' attorneys appealed on the grounds that the district court's order did not extend to other black students similarly situated, nor did it dismantle the Pupil Placement Board. The court of appeals found the plaintiffs' argument persuasive and, for the first time, reprimanded Richmond's school board for publicly shirking its responsibility while privately sanctioning the segregationist policies of a placement board, a creation of the state whose existence was unlawful at worst, untenable at best:

> Notwithstanding the fact that the Pupil Placement Board assigns pupils to various Richmond schools without recommendation of the local officials, we do not believe that the City School Board can disavow all responsibility for the maintenance of the discriminatory system which has apparently undergone no basic change since its adoption. . . . It would be foolish in the extreme to

say that neither the City School Board nor the Pupil Placement Board has the duty to recognize and protect the constitutional rights of pupils in the Richmond schools. . . . We are of the opinion that it is primarily the duty of the School Board to eliminate the offending system.[31]

It is important to understand that whether the assignment of pupils rested with a state placement board or a city school board, the mere fact that blacks themselves had to take the initiative to apply was undoubtedly one of the greatest drawbacks of any assignment plan. White local officials, most of whom were already on record in support of segregation, could hardly be expected to initiate desegregation. Therefore, it was always black parents, and never white parents, who had to volunteer to send their children out of their familiar surroundings and into "enemy territory." And if their children were assigned to a white school, the psychological burden then shifted from parent to child. Already burdened with feelings of inferiority and insecurity, black children were understandably reluctant to transfer to an alien and often hostile environment where racial prejudice and discrimination could become particularly acute. In fact, whites counted on that very thing to keep blacks out of their schools. Kenneth E. Whitlock, Jr., who attended Richmond's public schools from 1955 through 1967, had vivid recollections of his experiences as one of the first blacks to attend a white school. "At Chandler [Junior High] I was suddenly thrust into a white environment, and the racism I encountered, that Southern, rebel racism, was vehement. I can still remember once walking up the street to school with my black friends, and the white kids were waiting for us to come by. As we approached them they shouted, 'I smell a gar.' When we asked, 'what, a cigar?' they replied, 'no, a niggar.' I can still remember the humiliation I felt, knowing that people hated me because of my color, and that they thought I was subhuman."[32]

For these black youngsters getting their first inside look at the larger white society, the adjustment was a difficult one, and the psychological trauma associated with integration was almost overwhelming. And though all white teachers did not openly display racial prejudice towards black students, their attitudes towards blacks were generally condescending and indifferent, and their professional judgment was often affected by ingrained racial stereotypes and myths. Whitlock noted that his grades, as well as those of other good black students, "began to go down, almost across the board." He attributed this phenomenon to the white teachers' racial attitudes and the black students' lowered self-esteem. As an unspoken rule, blacks did not participate in extracurricular activities because the hostility that was so evident in the classroom usually became much more intense on the playing field, where blacks were easy targets for social ostracism and physical abuse. Equally disconcerting for Whitlock was the sudden realization that his middle–class upbringing not only had poorly prepared him to deal with racial bigotry but had in no way exempted him from it. "The fact that I came from a middle class background didn't make me any less vulnerable to the racial slurs that I heard daily, something which made me realize that all blacks, regardless of their socio-economic status, have the same feelings of powerlessness in a white-dominated, racist environment."[33]

Complicating matters further for these black pioneers was the tremendous psychological pressures they were under to succeed, which, unfortunately, came at a time when they were least likely to excel academically in an often hostile environment. They felt that the hope of future generations of black children rested with them, and if they failed to make any lasting impression on their white teachers and to prove to the world that they were capable of competing successfully with their white counterparts, white segregationists might finally have sufficient evidence to expose *Brown* as an unwarranted social experiment concocted by misguided liberals. In view of this psychological burden and numerous other contributing factors that made their experience at white schools so intolerable, it is no wonder that the vast majority of black students preferred to remain in their own schools.

During the period that the Pupil Placement Board was in operation, Richmond's school board's official policy was one of unquestioned compliance with state law. Virginia Crockford, a white member of the school board from 1962 to 1972, was convinced that the Pupil Placement Board was a ploy by the state "to buy time." One of the school board's most outspoken members, who was often maligned by the white community for her liberal views (and whose life was threatened on many occasions), Crockford regarded the Pupil Placement Board as "one of those nuisance things that you had to go along with because it was state law. Its purpose was to hamper school desegregation. They [the Virginia General Assembly] wouldn't have put it in had it been for anything else."[34]

Virginia Crockford was not the only school board member at the time who disagreed with the school board's policy regarding the state's pupil–assignment plan. Booker T. Bradshaw, the board's only black member who served from 1953 to 1965, expressed his disillusionment frequently but quietly, ever mindful of the social milieu in which he was operating. Born in St. Louis, Missouri in 1904, Bradshaw was, by most accounts, a product of his times—a man whose political views were very similar to those of his famous predecessor whose name he bore. Like Booker T. Washington, Bradshaw was an accommodationist who believed that blacks could make more progess if they adopted a gradualist rather than a militant approach. Although deeply committed to the fight for social justice, he did not believe that things would change overnight and felt that nothing could be accomplished by deliberately antagonizing whites. Even if he had wanted to do more, the fact that he was the sole black member on the school board during his twelve–year tenure meant that he was powerless to effect any real change in policy. In fact, Bradshaw's influence on the board, insofar as school desegregation was concerned, appears to have been negligible; his opinions might have been solicited, but the real decisions were made "around him at all-white private clubs."[35] Consequently, he had little choice but to go along with the agenda put forth by the white members. In any event, it is doubtful whether any other black would have had greater success in trying to encourage the school board to take more immediate action to desegregate the schools.

Lewis F. Powell, Jr., a partner in the law firm of Hunton, Williams, Gay, Powell and Gibson since 1937, and later an associate justice on the United States Supreme Court, served as chairman of Richmond's school board from 1952 to 1961 (he had been a board member since 1950). A Virginia native, Powell's roots were in a deeply segregated society. While maintaining that his was not a racist upbringing (his parents were devout Christians), he admits that in many respects he was a product of his segregationist environment. "I'm ashamed to say that I never questioned segregation until the Supreme Court decided that case [*Brown*]," Powell said in a 1986 interview. "*Plessy* was the law of the land. I was born and raised with separate laws. And that was a way of life. Now, I had a good many black friends, and I don't think anybody could honestly say that I was a racist. But I did accept the society in which I was born and raised, and I'm not at all proud of that."[36]

Powell was a Virginia Democrat, but felt free to vote Republican in national elections. He admired Senator Harry F. Byrd, Sr. because Byrd was a fiscal conservative and supported a strong national defense. On balance, Powell believes that the Byrd Machine gave Virginians honest government. He broke with Byrd over the issue of massive resistance, however, primarily because he believed that children, both black and white, would suffer irreparable harm if the state adopted such laws. His principal concern as school board chairman during this time was to keep Richmond's public schools open.[37]

Powell made a trip to Washington early in the massive–resistance crisis in an unsuccessful attempt to persuade Byrd to abandon his position. He also debated the issue with Richmond newspaper editor James J. Kilpatrick, who, along with many other segregationists, relied on the "doctrine of interposition" as the constitutional justification for their defiance. Powell believed that "if ever there had been [any] merit to [this] doctrine, it was relegated to history by the War between the States." Furthermore, Powell believed (as surprisingly few in the South did at this time) that the passage of the Thirteenth, Fourteenth, and Fifteenth Amendments to the Constitution rejected for all time the notion that each state could determine its own law without regard to the constitution.[38] Despite his efforts, Powell convinced few die-hard segregationists to alter their course of action and ultimately grew despondent over his unsuccessful mission. In a private letter to newsman Edward R. Murrow, Powell expressed his belief that "a climate of intolerance now exists in the South which, in my opinion, far exceeds, both in intensity and danger to our country, the type of intolerance which came to be known as McCarthyism."[39]

Though schools were closed in several Virginia localities, Powell takes pleasure in noting that he and his school–board colleagues succeeded in keeping Richmond's schools open. "I spent some agonizing years on the Richmond school board but in the end was glad that I had the opportunity to serve on it," Powell remarked some years later. In addition to his terms on Richmond's school board, Powell served the state in numerous other capacities, including eight years on the state board of education. He was equally proud of his membership in the Virginia Industrialization Group, an alliance of Virginia business, professional, and civic leaders chaired by Stuart Saunders and J. Harvie Wilkinson, Jr., that worked quietly to end massive resistance in Virginia. In reflecting upon his role and that of the school board during massive resistance, Powell commented:

> Had we attempted to integrate the schools in the early years, this would have resulted in closing the schools. The Richmond City Council that provided the funds to operate the public schools was stridently opposed to any integration. Both Richmond newspapers also opposed integration, as did Virginia governors, and the majority of the Virginia General Assembly, until finally the Virginia Supreme Court invalidated the massive–resistance laws.
>
> I do not suggest, however, that perhaps we should not have moved toward integration "with greater deliberate speed" than we believed was feasible at the time.[40]

Indeed, many have praised Lewis Powell for displaying respectable leadership as school board chairman, especially in light of the climate of hatred and fear that existed at the time. In a 1987 tribute to Powell, his longtime friend civil–rights attorney Oliver Hill made these observations: "He was a pioneer in promoting biracial support at a time when such cooperation was frowned upon by the political and business interests in our city. . . . In his work in local and state affairs, Lewis Powell has steadfastly pursued the twin goals of educational excellence and racial cooperation. Through the difficult period of the 1950s and even during his tenure as a Supreme Court Justice, his interest has been genuine, his commitment unfailing."[41]

A fair examination of the record, however, clearly shows that Richmond maintained a patently segregated system during Powell's administration. There is some disagreement, though, as to who was responsible for this—the school board or the Pupil Placement Board. Powell's eight-year tenure as chairman was characterized by overcrowded black public schools, white schools not filled to normal capacity, and the board's effective perpetuation of a discriminatory assignment system that trapped black children in inadequate segregated schools. As noted in the *Bradley* case, the Richmond School Board could not even maintain that a reasonable start had been made toward the elimination of racially discriminatory practices. In fact, only a few months after Powell left the school board, the fourth circuit court found that "the system of dual attendance areas which has operated over the years to maintain public schools on a racially segregated basis has been permitted to continue. . . . Rather than admitting that it had failed, the Richmond School Board was blaming the 'Pupil Placement Board' and others for what was clearly its own miserable dereliction of duty."[42]

It thus became apparent to advocates of desegregation that without a class–action suit and heavy pressure on the school board, segregation would continue. By the fall of 1963, for example, out of more than 26,000 blacks in Richmond schools, only 312 were enrolled in twelve white schools. Roy Wilkins told the 1963 state NAACP convention that "Virginia has the largest and most successful token integration plan in the country," but he added that blacks would not be satisfied "with even the best tokenism." Richmond perfectly fit these generalizations about the state.[43]

In the spring of 1963, attorneys Samuel W. Tucker and Henry L. Marsh III, the newest member of the Hill and Tucker law firm, launched a new offensive to desegregate Richmond's schools. Specifically, they objected to two key features of the city's public–school system—dual attendance zones and the "feeder" system—that greatly facilitated the Pupil Placement Board's policy and, consequently, severely hampered desegregation. Attendance zones were prescribed geographic boundaries, usually drawn along residential neighborhoods, that determined which school each child would attend. Under the feeder system, children were automatically assigned from certain elementary schools to certain junior high schools and then to specified high schools. Under Richmond's system, white schools "fed" other white schools and black schools "fed" other black schools. Both practices, Tucker and Marsh argued, were patently discriminatory.[44]

In March 1963, the attorneys won a court order requiring the school board to abolish the system of feeder schools and dual attendance zones. In June, the school board adopted a new policy that would allow students greater choice in their selection of schools. Once a student made his or her request, the school board would then recommend each child's assignment according to residence, available space in the schools, the educational programs offered, and "what is deemed to be in the best interest of such pupil." These recommendations were then to be forwarded to the Pupil Placement Board. The school board unanimously adopted the new plan, which was scheduled to go into effect by the fall term of 1963.[45]

Response to this new plan was mixed. Board member Booker T. Bradshaw said he interpreted the plan as a "freedom of choice plan," which meant that "no undue barriers will be placed before a child" seeking transfer. "If a child wants to transfer . . . and gives legitimate reasons, we can't set up barriers." Superintendent Henry I. Willett agreed that it was "freedom of choice within limits. . . . It doesn't mean any child anywhere can get into any school without [meeting] these criteria." Frank S. Calkins, vice-chairman of the board, said he voted for the measure because he was "obliged to . . . but I must say I'm perfectly happy with the situation as it is now."[46]

The significance of this new "freedom of choice" plan was that although the Pupil Placement Board was still technically charged with the responsibility of assigning pupils to the city's schools, increasing pressure from the courts had forced the city school administration to act more independently of the Pupil Placement Board and to take a more active role in the assignment procedure, that, in turn, forced it to facilitate at least a modest undermining of the segregation system. Equally important, the school board retained such broad discretion in the matter of assignments that it was able to resist any uniform policy which might result in wholesale integration. "Freedom of choice" came into its own with abundant safe-guards intact.

On August 28, 1963, Tucker and Marsh returned to court, dissatisfied with the school board–approved plan. The centerpiece of their argument was that not only would students wishing to transfer from one school to another still have to go through the racist Pupil Placement Board but that the problem of segregated faculty had not been addressed. Further, they argued that the new plan contained no provisions for desegregation of special programs for the handicapped and the gifted, nor would it allow for any desegregation of adult education programs and specialized courses. This "new plan," they contended, sounded a lot better than it really was. Despite these protests, on March 16, 1964, District Judge John Butzner approved the school board's "freedom–of–choice" plan. On appeal, the fourth circuit court affirmed the decision, stating that the freedom of choice plan satisfied the school board's constitutional obligations.[47] The plaintiffs appealed to the United States Supreme Court.

Between Butzner's ruling of March 1964 and the fourth circuit court's decision upholding it in April 1965, other developments took place that accelerated the pace of desegregation in the South. The most significant of these was the passage of the Civil Rights Act of 1964. Title II forbade discrimination in all public accommodations, which included restaurants and lunch counters, motels and hotels, sports arenas and theaters. Of more immediate importance, new desegregation guidelines established under the Department of Health, Education, and Welfare stipulated that the federal government would cut off funds to recalcitrant school districts. In conjunction with these new guidelines, the Civil Rights Act permitted the Department of Justice to file suit "for the orderly achievement of desegregation in public education."[48] This came as a welcome relief to the NAACP, whose legal staff had almost singlehandedly shouldered the burden of legal challenges to segregation since 1954. But the Justice Department's involvement in school desegregation meant much more than legal assistance. Its mere presence meant that the federal government was finally prepared to take a stand on the issue, and that the judiciary might finally be able to count on the executive and legislative branches for legal initiative as well as moral support.

Meanwhile, the Supreme Court was still deliberating the issue of freedom of choice and how it might most effectively be implemented. The Court apparently understood that if freedom of choice were to be meaningful, both faculty and student desegregation had to occur. White students would not attend schools with all-black faculties, and few white teachers cared to teach only black children. As J. Harvie Wilkinson III has noted, "For a school to be identifiably black in any way—by the composition of its student body, faculty, or staff, even by its school name or traditions—was the surest way to stiffen white resistance to attending it."[49] Therefore, on November 15, 1965, the Supreme Court ruled that Judge Butzner had erred in approving a desegregation plan for Richmond without addressing assertions of racial bias in faculty assignments, and reversed the decision of the court of appeals. In a companion case, the Court warned that racial segregation of teachers would invalidate an otherwise constitutional pupil–desegregation plan.[50]

Acting in accordance with the decision of the Supreme Court, the district court held the required hearing concerning faculty assignments and, on March 30, 1966, approved a revised freedom–of–choice plan submitted by the school board and agreed to by the plaintiffs. According to this plan, the school board recognized "its responsibility to promote and discharge teachers and other personnel without regard to race or color." It also stated that if the steps taken by the school board "do not produce significant results during the 1966–67 school year, it is recognized that the freedom of choice plan will have to be modified." This plan remained in operation for nearly five years.[51]

Brown was now eleven years old, but school desegregation in Richmond continued to move at a snail's pace. Despite favorable rulings by the federal courts, black children in Richmond wanting to attend desegregated schools with whites still had to obtain local permission, which, ever since the admission of the first two blacks in 1960, had been granted to only a handful of black children whose parents had had the courage and dogged persistence to request that their children be assigned to white schools. But now, with the courts' approval of a new desegregation plan—freedom of choice—it appeared as if a new era was dawning throughout the entire country. Freedom of choice sounded fair enough. But could it realistically dismantle Richmond's dual school system? That remained to be seen.

THREE

A Myth in Operation:
The Era of Freedom of Choice, 1966–71

Richmond was so residentially segregated that it frustrated all future
attempts to desegregate the public schools. That was perhaps the major
reason why freedom of choice never worked. Many people wondered
why we [the NAACP] didn't tackle segregated housing before we tackled
segregated schools. Personally, I was in favor of that strategy, because if
we could desegregate the housing then blacks could go to the desegregated neighborhood schools. But judging from the experiences of some
places where violence had erupted whenever blacks moved into white
neighborhoods, we felt that it might be safer to proceed with school
desegregation first, assuming that kids would be less violent than adults.
I've always believed that the children could have worked out many of the
problems associated with school desegregation if only their parents had
left them alone.

—Oliver W. Hill (veteran civil–rights attorney)

The Pupil Placement Board, which had assigned most of Virginia's
children to their public schools over the previous ten years, was allowed to
expire by Virginia's General Assembly, effective June 30, 1966. Dr.
Earnest J. Oglesby, a Charlottesville segregationist who had been chairman
of that board since 1960, was proud of his service and appeared to be
greatly disappointed by the board's demise. He admitted that "voluntary
integration just wasn't working. The Negroes just weren't asking to go to
school with the whites, at least not in numbers sufficient to satisfy the
federal government."[1] His statement seems to indicate that apparently no
one ever seriously considered that whites would voluntarily choose to
attend schools with blacks. From the very outset, then, it was evident that

any pupil–assignment plan, no matter how fair it sounded, would require a bold initiative on the part of the black community if school desegregation were to succeed. As it turned out, such an initiative was not forthcoming. As the struggle for desegregation continued, it became increasingly clear that the same lack of administrative leadership that had doomed earlier pupil–assignment plans would also frustrate freedom of choice, which, after all, was predicated on the same premise. But then perhaps that was the idea from the very beginning.

In April 1966 Richmond's freedom–of–choice plan went into effect. Beginning with the 1966–67 school year, all parents with children in the public schools received a form on which they indicated which school they wanted their children to attend. Parents were free to choose any school in the city, provided that the curriculum was suitable and space was available. Parents had a thirty-day period in which to make their choice, beginning on April 1. Finally, the plan contained the provision that all personnel assignments would be made on a non-racial, nondiscriminatory basis.[2]

Henry L. Marsh, counsel for the black plaintiffs, said that the agreement was a consensus of all the parties and that it represented a "turning point in the long struggle to fully desegregate the Richmond public school system." Marsh hastened to add, though, that the plan "will be judged by the results it produces rather than by the wording of the principles expressed therein." It was not long, however, before the limitations inherent in freedom of choice were exposed.[3]

Concerned that the federal government was pushing too hard for desegregation, Governor Mills E. Godwin, Jr., met with top federal officials to protest the new HEW guidelines. A former massive resister who once referred to integration as "a cancer eating at the very life blood of our public school system," Godwin contended that some of the requirements of the new freedom–of–choice plan, such as the enforced desegregation of faculties, seemed unnecessarily rigid. Nor was he convinced that the federal government had the authority under the Civil Rights Act of 1964 to try to achieve a racial balance in the schools. "It must be recognized that full desegregation of an historical dual public school system based on traditional social patterns . . . cannot be achieved by federal edicts in a relatively short span of time without serious disruption in the efficient operation of that school system," Godwin said.[4]

When Richmond's schools opened in September 1966, 44,362 pupils were enrolled. Of that number, 28,529 (64.3 percent) were black. And though a few more black students had enrolled in previously all-white schools, the numbers were not nearly as high as blacks had hoped for. Faculty desegregation was even more disappointing. Superintendent Willett told city council members that there was a "reluctance on the part of both white and Negro teachers to cross over to schools of the opposite race," making faculty desegregation a painfully slow process. Willett told council, "We lost some good teacher prospects of both races because they were not assured of teaching in schools that were predominantly of their own race." He added that the school administration "used persuasion, and not force, in attempting to place teachers in a school of the opposite race."[5] But when persuasion failed, as it often did, the administration generally refused to consider other options.

All state and local officials from the governor on down tried to limit the scope of freedom of choice in every way possible. One of their most common (and most effective) ploys was to try to convince black parents that their children's interests could best be served by remaining in their own schools. For example, one of the provisions of the freedom–of–choice plan stipulated that once black parents made the decision to transfer their children to white schools, their request was filed with the school board and their decision was irrevocable. Undoubtedly the main purpose of this provision was to convince black parents that they should think long and hard before transferring their children out of their traditional schools where their race predominated into schools in which they constituted a distinct minority.

Because black parents had fought so hard to have their children admitted to white schools, one may wonder why some of them began to question the wisdom of their earlier judgment. The reasons for their sudden disillusionment with freedom of choice were many. At a meeting of the Southside Virginia Institute on Desegregation held at the University of Virginia in July 1967, several school administrators noted that the number of black students choosing to attend all-white schools was rapidly decreasing and pointed to several deficiencies in the freedom–of–choice plan. The administrators cited some specific reasons why blacks were apprehensive about choosing white schools, the primary one being "a subtle type of harassment of the children at a time when there was no teacher supervision," such as on school buses and on the playgrounds. Another reason was the "language of prejudice," in which certain words carried derogatory connotations, even in the case of younger blacks. Finally, there was a simple reluctance on the part of black students to leave their familiar surroundings in order to attend white schools where they knew they were not welcome.[6] As one black parent put it, "you had to be a rather courageous kid to go [to a white school], particularly when your reception might not be friendly. I still think children are more charitable than adults, but they can be awfully mean at times."[7]

Because many Richmond blacks were domestics and laborers, the vast majority of whom depended upon whites for their jobs, the possibility of arbitrary termination of employment clearly existed for those who voiced a preference for integration. Based on the experiences of those who were actively involved in the efforts to desegregate, these fears were real, not imagined. Oliver Hill recalled that many blacks were threatened, and some were actually fired, for expressing their support for desegregation. Blacks who agreed to be plaintiffs in lawsuits aimed at ending segregation could almost certainly expect some form of economic reprisal. The mere threat itself was sometimes sufficient to prevent blacks from exercising their options under the freedom–of–choice plan.[8]

Perhaps the greatest obstacle to school desegregation under freedom of choice was residential segregation. Richmond's housing patterns contained well-defined black and white neighborhoods. These vestiges of the city's history of racial segregation and discrimination could, by and large, be attributed directly to the actions of the state and federal government. Before 1964, public housing projects were built according to racial identity and were established specifically for either black or white occupancy. This segregation had been sanctioned by discriminatory Federal Housing Authority (FHA) regulations. Up until the time that it became a part of the Department of Housing and Urban Development (HUD), the FHA refused to insure home loans in those areas that were not racially homogeneous. So discriminatory were Richmond's housing policies in 1968 when the city applied to HUD for a Model Neighborhood Planning Grant for the purpose of renovating its black community, city officials themselves acknowledged that Richmond's residential pattern had been developed in a manner that had resulted in "a total isolation and segregation of the Negro."[9]

When state-sanctioned discrimination began to disappear as a result of increasing black protest, whites turned to restrictive covenants. Prior to the passage of the federal Fair Housing Act of 1968, most subdivision deeds in Richmond included racially restrictive covenants. It was commonplace for the city to purchase for use by the school board land for which the deed contained racially restrictive covenants. Perhaps the best evidence of the entrenched custom of racial discrimination in housing is that real estate ads appearing in the city's newspapers, even as late as 1968, continued to designate which houses were for "colored." These covenants had long-term effects on Richmond's black community by helping to foster the notion of separate and unequal development in housing as well as other areas of public policy. Such conditions greatly frustrated the disestablishment of segregated schools.[10]

During Richmond's era of freedom of choice, children had three ways of getting to school: they could walk, get their parents to take them, or pay to ride the city buses operated by the Virginia Transit Company. At the time, there were no free yellow school buses operating in the city. Consequently, except for a handful of black children who lived close enough to white schools to walk, transferring from a black to a white school presented a number of practical difficulties. Because of the constraints imposed by their jobs, most blacks simply could not accept the full-time responsibility of taking their children to school in the morning and picking them up in the afternoon, nor could they afford the expense of having their children ride city buses to school. Dr. Francis Foster, a black dentist and civil rights activist in Richmond, remembered that most blacks could not take advantage of freedom of choice, because of transportation problems. "When my oldest daughter, Carmen, decided to go to Thomas Jefferson [a white high school] I had to take her myself," recalled Foster. "It was her decision to go, but it was my responsibility to provide transportation."[11] Because Foster was a self-employed professional, his flexible work schedule enabled him to drive his daughter to school. Most Richmond blacks did not have that option.

White parents, on the other hand, had a different set of choices to make. When certain previously all-white schools, because of their geographic location, began to enroll increasing numbers of blacks, many white parents withdrew their children from those schools and enrolled them in other white schools. Hence, in areas where schools were located near the borders of black and white neighborhoods, a period of desegregation was followed by a period of *resegregation*. To cite one extreme example, J. E. B. Stuart Elementary School, all-white in 1962, had 761 blacks and only 12 whites in 1966.[12]

In early 1968 a group of educators began a study of the effects of school desegregation in Richmond. Headed by Dr. James A. Sartain, a professor of sociology at the University of Richmond, this urban–study team focused on Richmond's northside, an area that had been losing a substantial number of white residents to the suburbs and was undergoing a major conversion from white to black, which was being reflected in the school population as well as the larger neighborhood. The team was directed to identify the causes of this resegregation and to make recommendations as to how this phenomenon might be avoided in other areas of the city. In November the team submitted part of its report. Entitled *Implications and Recommendations of Urban Team Study on Northside Schools* (generally referred to as the Sartain Report), the report stated that resegregation in many of Richmond's neighborhoods was already well under way. In order for the city to overcome racial imbalance, Richmond's public school system would eventually have to merge with those of Henrico and Chesterfield, the two overwhelmingly white counties bordering the city. The team members acknowledged that their study might have been undertaken "several years too late to prevent the resegregation of the schools in the Northside but it is certainly not too late to give serious consideration to the future of schools in the rest of Richmond or, indeed, in the rest of the country."[13]

The study team further observed that within some desegregated schools students seemed to be polarized along racial lines, resulting in the exclusion of blacks from certain organizations. The team cited several instances where racial discrimination was apparent, such as predominantly black athletic teams with all-white coaching staffs and some predominantly black schools with no black guidance counselors. In the case of black students, their color always seemed to be the overriding issue and, unfortunately, the major impediment, in gaining acceptance in a predominantly white setting:

> The problem is compounded and seems to be more crucial in this Negro migration than in other group movements. In other group movements there was no discriminative color factor to demonstrate the mobility as clearly as in the present situation. The Negro mobility and desire for better housing and schools may be following the historic process, but is more noticeable because of color differences. The same color factor may be operating in school desegregation or school resegregation issues. When the Italian or Irish youngsters entered the schools in large numbers there was no easy way to distinguish them from the people already in the schools. However, as the Negroes enter the schools, perhaps in no larger numbers than when other large groups entered the schools, it is easy to spot and define a "color line."[14]

An interesting paradox noted by the team was that "procedures which will encourage desegregation and alleviate some of the perceived problems of the Negro youth and parents in the schools will at the same time encourage resegregation in the schools." As more black teachers, coaches, and administrators were assigned to predominantly white schools, black student enrollment increased. But when the black enrollment at any school began to approach 40 percent of the overall student population, whites felt their "comfort zone" being threatened; hence, many white parents began requesting transfers or leaving the neighborhood, thus resegregating the school.[15]

Meanwhile, another important case was making its way toward the Supreme Court. In New Kent, a small, rural county in eastern Virginia, blacks made up 57 percent of the school population. The county had only two schools—white New Kent in the eastern part and black George W. Watkins in the west. For more than a decade after *Brown,* schools in New Kent had remained totally segregated. To remain eligible for federal funds following passage of the 1964 Civil Rights Act, the county adopted a freedom–of–choice plan in August 1965. The plan worked about as well as could be expected. Black enrollment in formerly all–white New Kent increased from 35 in 1965 to 111 in 1966 to 115 in 1967. In 1967, one white teacher was employed at Watkins and one black taught at New Kent. But no white students chose to attend all-black Watkins, where, despite freedom of choice, 85 percent of the county's black schoolchildren were still enrolled.[16]

The case of *Green v. County School Board of New Kent County* was decided by the Supreme Court in 1968. In one of the most significant school–desegregation decisions since *Brown,* the Court ruled that the freedom–of–choice concept was unconstitutional so long as a basically dual school system resulted. Mere "deliberate speed" was no longer sufficient. At last, the Court removed from blacks the onus of initiating school desegregation and placed it with local school boards. "The burden on a school today," the Court said in *Green,* "is to come forward with a plan that promises realistically to work, and promises realistically to work *now.*" The Court stopped short of concluding that freedom of choice would never work, but did emphasize the point that New Kent's plan was not acceptable as long as 85 percent of the county's black children remained in an all-black school.[17]

On March 10, 1970, attorneys for the plaintiffs in Richmond's ongoing school–desegregation case filed a motion for further relief in view of the Court's opinion in *Green.* They argued that Richmond's freedom–of–choice plan, in effect for four years, had failed to convert the public schools into nonsegregated, unitary systems. Enrollment figures validated their assertion. As of May 1, 1970, Richmond's public–school system enrolled approximately 52,000 students. Of the seven high schools, three were 100 percent black; one was 99.3 percent white; one was 92 percent white; one, 81 percent white; and one, 68 percent black. For the nine middle schools, two were 100 percent black; one was 99.9 percent black; one was 88 percent black; one was 73 percent black; one was 69 percent black; three were 91 percent or more white (91 percent, 97 percent, and 98 percent). In the forty-four elementary schools, seventeen were 100 percent black; four others were more than 93 percent black; one was 78 percent black; two schools were 100 percent white; thirteen others were 90 percent or more white; two were roughly 86 percent white; and five were between 53 percent and 70 percent white. The figures for faculty and staff were even more lopsided. If freedom of choice had indeed been designed to promote desegregation, it clearly had fallen way short of the mark.[18]

In response to the plaintiffs' motion, the Richmond School Board adopted a new desegregation plan drawn up by HEW. The plan called for "grade pairing," which would allow for black and white schools in the same attendance zone to be "paired," with each school containing different grade levels. (For example, the former "white school" in a particular district would now serve both white and black students in kindergarten through grade six, and the former "black school" would serve both white and black students in grades seven through twelve.) The major drawback of this plan, however, was that it was feasible only when black and white schools were in close proximity to each other, which was rarely the case. Residential segregation was a fact of life for much of the city, but was particularly acute in two areas, namely the annexed area and the east end. Those two areas accounted for twenty-three of the city's seventy-three public schools and special education centers. Under the proposed plan, the annexed area schools would have an enrollment of 8,017 whites and only 206 blacks. East end schools would enroll 13,745 blacks and only 374 whites (see table 1). Without transportation, children in segregated neighborhoods would be unable to gain access to schools in other neighborhoods.[19]

Table 1. Racial composition of schools in the East End and the Annexed Area under Plan I, approved in May 1970

School	Grades	White	Black
	East End		
Kennedy	9-12	223	1,641
East End	8-9	52	728
Armstrong	9-12	73	1,637
Mosby	K-9	7	2,436
Bacon	K-6	3	866
Bellevue	K-6	3	306
Bowler	K-6	0	646
Chimborazo	K-7	3	855
Fairfield	K-7	0	819
Fairmount	K-6	0	925
Mason	K-7	0	1,061
Whitcomb	K-6	10	871
Woodville	K-7	0	954
	Annexed Area		
Huguenot	10-12	1,344	10
Elkhardt	7-9	762	25
Thompson	7-9	1,388	26
Broad Rock	K-6	491	12
Fisher	K-6	709	0
Francis	K-6	502	13
Greene	K-6	477	59
Redd	K-6	541	0
Reid	K-6	1,056	21
Southampton	K-6	747	40

Source: Richmond Public Schools, City Hall, Richmond, Va.

The fact that one area was predominantly black and the other predominantly white was not the only feature distinguishing the east end from the

annexed area. Unlike the former, the latter had only recently become a part
of the city of Richmond, and hence, was still referred to as such. In May
1969 a compromise line was approved by Richmond and Chesterfield
County, which resulted in the city being awarded twenty-three square miles
of land formerly belonging to Chesterfield. The preannexation population
of the city was 202,359, of which 104,207, or 52 percent, were black. The
annexation added to the city 47,262 new citizens, of whom only 1,557 were
black and 45,705 were white. The postannexation population of the city
was therefore 249,621, of which 105,764, or 42 percent, were black. The
annexation became effective on January 1, 1970.[20]

Although Richmond's white politicians maintained that the annexation
was necessary in order to expand the city's tax base, blacks charged that the
annexation was racially motivated, and that its sole purpose was to dilute
black voting strength by reducing Richmond's black population from a 52
percent majority to a 42 percent minority. In light of the disingenuous
tactics used by Richmond's white leaders, most notably their ability to
conduct annexation negotiations with Chesterfield officials in secrecy for
six years—negotiations that were seemingly devoid of financial considerations—it would appear that black leaders were correct in arguing that the
city and county were engaging in racial politics. In fact, remarks made by
Richmond's mayor Phil J. Bagley, who was quoted as saying, "I don't want
niggers to take over the city," were clearly indicative of the city's underlying motive.[21] Years later, when a series of suits protesting the annexation
reached the United States Supreme Court, Justice William J. Brennan noted
that:

> Richmond's focus in the negotiations was upon the number of new white
> voters it could obtain by annexation; it expressed no interest in economic or
> geographic considerations such as tax revenues, vacant land, utilities, or
> schools. The record is replete with statements by Richmond officials which
> prove beyond question that the predominant (if not the sole) motive and desire
> of the negotiators of the 1969 settlement was to acquire 44,000 additional
> white citizens for Richmond in order to avert a transfer of political control to
> what was fast becoming a black–population majority.[22]

Whatever the city's motives might have been, the annexation not only
temporarily undermined the city's black majority, but it also added another
dimension to Richmond's historical pattern of residential segregation.

On June 26, 1970, District Court Judge Robert R. Merhige, Jr., advised
the school board that Richmond's history of residential segregation rendered the proposed "pairing plan" unacceptable:

> It is patently obvious that school construction and faculty assignments,
> coupled with all of the other discriminatory practices engaged in and encour-
> aged by local, state and federal agencies, as well as private discriminatory

practices, require that the plan submitted be disapproved by this Court on the ground that, while the assignment of pupils to neighborhood schools is undoubtedly both a sound and desirable concept, it cannot in the Circuit be approved if residence in a neighborhood is denied to Negro pupils solely on the ground of color, as this Court has found.

Unfortunately it would appear that in spite of the lifting of public discriminatory practices as a result of the repeal of White supremacy laws, congressional action and judicial pronouncements, no real hope for the dismantling of dual school systems appears to be in the offing unless and until there is a dismantling of the all-Black residential areas.[23]

On July 23, the school board submitted to the court a second desegregation plan. Although this plan provided for pairing, pupil assignments, majority to minority transfers, and some transportation (mainly of the indigent), the court held that this plan was also unacceptable, primarily because almost nine thousand black students would continue to attend thirteen elementary schools that were 90 percent or more black, while four schools would remain all white. These concerns notwithstanding, the court, at an August 7 hearing, approved Plan II on an interim basis because the school year was scheduled to begin in two weeks. But the court concluded that the second plan, like the first, clearly failed to convert Richmond's dual school system into a unitary one, and that a third plan would have to be submitted within ninety days.[24]

When schools opened on August 31, 1970, under the interim desegregation plan, the enrollment figures were quite shocking: nearly five thousand white students were missing. Out of a projected enrollment of 21,139 white students, only 16,429 were enrolled on opening day. By contrast, 28,011 blacks of the 28,975 predicted to attend were present. A large number of whites who were absent from school lived south of the James River, the area most affected by the city's new desegregation arrangements. And though the limited busing plan was aimed primarily at the high schools, white absenteeism at elementary schools was just as high. In the elementary schools, where more than 1,800 white pupils were missing, figures indicate that whites who were assigned to schools where they would have been in a very small minority simply did not attend. For example, Fairmount Elementary was supposed to have twelve white pupils, but not a single one enrolled.[25]

At the high school level, some of the white absenteeism was attributed to the "senior option" aspect of the city's desegregation plan, which allowed seniors to remain at the schools they had attended the previous year. Hence, a significant percentage of white seniors who would otherwise have been transferred to schools with large black populations elected to remain at their predominantly white schools. Yet, senior option could not account for the high rate of white absenteeism at the other high school grades. At traditionally white high schools like Thomas Jefferson, Huguenot, and John Marshall, only 181 more seniors than predicted were enrolled, not nearly enough to explain the absence of 1,140 white students assigned to traditionally black high schools: namely, Armstrong, Kennedy, and Walker. Armstrong, which had the highest white absentee rate, had only 254 of its projected 685 white students.

It is clear that the high absentee rate among white students in the fall of 1970 reflected a growing opposition to the use of busing as a means of achieving school desegregation. Yet, out of 50,000 students, only 13,000 were being bused under the interim plan, the vast majority of these coming from the upper grade levels. Since the busing of white middle–school and high–school students had resulted in such disaffection, the busing of white elementary students would undoubtedly cause untold disruption in the city's public school system. Because the courts had already found the existing desegregation plan unacceptable, there was little doubt that the next plan would have to provide for much more extensive transportation if it was to comply with the courts' mandate of "meaningful desegregation," ambiguous though that term was. It was becoming evident that the white exodus from Richmond's public schools would only intensify, for within a period of three months the schools had gone from 60 percent black to 65 percent black.[26]

Many white parents soon resorted to a variety of schemes designed to keep their children out of the city's schools. The Richmond *News Leader* reported that some of the schemes were "legal, some illegal, some extra-legal, [and] many involve heavy financial sacrifice. Some are downright ingenious." Temporary guardianships, whereby children moved in with relatives or friends who resided in the neighboring counties, was one of the most commonly used tactics. Other strategies included renting apartments and establishing residences in county school districts, filing false addresses, and enrolling in private schools. The *News Leader* cited several interesting examples:

> A Richmond blue collar worker with school-age daughters 16 and 8 had a young married daughter living in Chesterfield County. Father and daughter simply switched domiciles. She moved into his home; he and his family moved into the daughter's apartment and took over her lease. His younger daughters now attend Chesterfield Schools.
>
> A girl rented an apartment in a white area of the city in her father's name to avoid transfer to predominantly black John F. Kennedy High School. The rent is paid and the girl goes to the apartment occasionally to see if there is any mail there for her from the school.
>
> A middle-income white collar worker took $3,000 from his college savings fund to enroll his teen-aged sons in a private school.
>
> A Richmond physician, to avoid predominantly black schools in his area, found openings in three separate private schools for three of his children. He

could find no opening for the fourth child, who is attending John Marshall
High School.

A South Richmond lawyer, to avoid having his two school-agers bused to
the city's East End, moved out of his house and rented an apartment in Chesterfield County. It is costing him about $125 a month for rent and utilities, but
he figures that is cheaper than private schools. After being contacted by the
police and school officials, the man remained defiant. "I don't care what the
federal government tells me; I'll go to jail if I have to; I'll move to the
Alleghanies if I have to; I'll move to South Africa; I'm tired of living by
minority rule," the lawyer said.

A North Side couple set up a false address in the West End so their son
could continue at Thomas Jefferson instead of transferring to John Marshall.

A South Richmond father dutifully drove his child seven miles each
morning after school opened to a Chesterfield County school bus pickup point.
He did so for six weeks, while waiting for a new baby to be born. When the
baby came, he sold his Richmond home and bought one in the county.

A Richmond couple rents an apartment near Thomas Jefferson High
School to keep their child in that school and to avoid Kennedy. Father and
mother take turns staying at the apartment with their child.

The *News Leader* reported that there were "many more examples" and that
those cited were "chosen arbitrarily as typical." School officials from
Richmond, Henrico, and Chesterfield reported that they had several ways of
finding out about such illegalities, but that one of their best sources of
information was from "tips" provided by jealous neighbors who resented
seeing some parents beat the system while their own children were being
bused off to predominantly black schools.[27]

The day after Richmond's schools opened under the interim busing
plan, several students were asked to comment on the new situation. As one
might expect, reactions were mixed. A senior [race not mentioned] called
the new situation "excellent." "I don't think there should be any question
about it. There's a difference and one I'm very happy about. . . . If left
to themselves students would find a solution [to integration] in their own
isolated sphere—the school. When you come to parents, that's the block.
They're holding it up." Michael Williams, a black student, said "The
people are helpful. I think it'll work out." White student Jay Clowes called
busing "great." "It's new to everybody and all it takes is an open mind. .
. . Out of 37 people in one class, I'm the only white person, but it's nice.
Nobody gives me any trouble."[28]

These optimists did not speak for everyone. Many black students
complained that white students kept to themselves and refused to associate
with them. Black student Denise Mack said she preferred to have her
school "all-black, as it had been in the past. It is plain to see that some
whites don't want to come here, and some of the black students would
rather that they not be here either." Another black student who asked to

remain anonymous said that he did not like the present arrangement, although he might change his mind later in the year. "White should be with white and black should be with black. Half of them [the white students] act funny and prissy anyway. They must think they are too good to associate with us." Some white students agreed that separation was the best policy. "I don't like it myself," said one white boy. "I don't like niggers and I don't like busing either—too many niggers on the buses. They walk around with switchblades and all." A white girl echoed his sentiments. "There are better schools [in] other places. The colored boys say smart things. They say 'Hello, sweetheart.' They try to touch you and that stuff. The only reason I came here was to keep my mother from being locked up."[29]

If the students had some misgivings about desegregation, as clearly many of them did, then their parents could hardly be expected to be any less concerned. At a school board meeting on September 17 a group of angry white parents complained that their children were the victims of "shakedowns" and other forms of violence and intimidation. One parent even demanded that federal troops be assigned to Elkhardt to protect white students there. Specifically, the parents called for an end to white "sprinkling" at Mosby Middle School and John F. Kennedy High School and vowed to appeal to the federal courts to have Merhige's desegregation order overturned. They argued that the plan created overcrowding in some classrooms, book shortages in places, a curtailment of extracurricular activities, and a serious decline in quality education.[30]

Whereas most white parents were concerned about the lack of discipline in the schools, most black parents were dissatisfied with the present transportation arrangements, noting that free transportation was still not being provided for the majority of the schoolchildren. Mrs. Betty C. Caleb, a black parent representing the Maymont Civic League, presented a petition calling for free transportation for all students and additional transportation for those engaged in extracurricular activities. Other black parents agreed, arguing that transportation placed a "financial strain" on many families. But whites balked at the suggestion that busing be implemented on a broader scale, at least insofar as their children were concerned. Mrs. Melvin Lubman, a white parent with children at Kennedy and Mosby, where whites were 7 percent and 4 percent of the schools' populations, respectively, said that when white children were assigned to black schools in very small numbers, the whites "melt away like snowflakes in July." Asserting that white children were being "isolated socially, culturally and racially," she urged the school board to "show some initiative, some moral fiber, some courage, the same qualities you are demanding of our young children—to go to court and ask for authority . . . to put our children back with their classmates."[31]

Less than two months later the school board did in fact return to court—but for reasons totally different from what most were expecting. On November 4, Richmond's school board filed a motion to make the school boards of Henrico and Chesterfield counties, as well as the Virginia State Board of Education, parties to the litigation. The city school board argued that increasing white flight to the suburbs was making school desegregation in Richmond impossible, and that the only solution was to merge the city schools with those of the counties, thereby creating a single metropolitan school system where blacks would make up one-third of the school population, rather than the two–thirds they presently accounted for in the city schools. Only then, the city school board argued, could real integration take place.[32]

Richmond's school board, having been expanded from five members to seven in January 1970, and now consisting of three blacks, was convinced that white flight was making it less likely that Richmond could achieve a desegregated school system within the context of increasing metropolitan polarization. The latest enrollment figures showed that of 15,439 black elementary pupils, 10,312 were in schools that were 90 percent or more black; and of 9,051 white elementary pupils, 4,138 were in schools that were 90 percent or more white. And of the nearly 5,000 white students who were absent from school in September, fewer than 500 had returned.[33]

Furthermore, Merhige's interim busing plan, limited though it was, had imposed a great economic strain on the city. Additional buses had to be purchased in order to meet the court's desegregation requirements, and because Judge Merhige had already determined that this plan would not dismantle Richmond's segregated system, it was a foregone conclusion that a more extensive busing plan was imminent. Metropolitan desegregation would not only shift much of that financial burden to the counties but would also minimize the amount of busing required for Richmond students, since the heaviest transportation would now fall on white students in Henrico and Chesterfield. Judge Merhige, who in fact had suggested the possibility of a merger as early as the summer of 1969, agreed that there was a constitutional basis for such a move. Therefore, on December 5, 1970, Merhige ruled that the adjoining counties of Henrico and Chesterfield, as well as the Virginia State Board of Education, had an affirmative duty to assist Richmond in desegregating its public schools and, consequently, should be made parties to the litigation. But it would be three years before the issue of metropolitan consolidation would finally be resolved. Judge Merhige, meanwhile, had other ideas.[34]

Growing increasingly dissatisfied with the lack of progress being made toward school desegregation, Judge Merhige began to search for viable alternatives and studied with great interest the busing decision that had been handed down in Charlotte, North Carolina, a few months earlier. In *Swann v. Charlotte-Mecklenburg Board of Education,* the first school busing case to reach the Supreme Court, the Court had approved the use of extensive busing to promote school desegregation. Merhige acknowledged the extent to which residential segregation had limited children's access to traditional white schools and was convinced that busing was the only way to achieve school desegregation in Richmond. The majority of white Richmonders, however, believed otherwise, and the fight over this highly volatile issue soon intensified on both sides.[35]

In January 1971 Merhige ruled that the level of desegregation achieved under the 1970–71 plan was "less than remarkable," and that "the Court is convinced that the student body compositions projected for the elementary schools under this plan betray a continuation of segregated education." He continued: "Moreover, the Court has determined that further delays in affording the plaintiffs what these defendants owe them under the Constitution . . . cannot be justified either by precedent or by practicality. . . . The Constitution is satisfied only when an integration plan 'works' in practice and not merely on paper."[36]

On April 5, 1971, a new era dawned in Richmond's history of public education. Judge Merhige ordered into effect a new desegregation plan, later affirmed by the Supreme Court, that provided for pupil and faculty reassignments and free citywide transportation. The new plan stipulated that pupils would have to be assigned so that the ratio of black to white in each school would be approximately the same as it was in the entire school system. Teacher assignments were to be made in a similar manner. Of far greater significance, though, was Merhige's decision to extend busing to all pupils within the city, including kindergarten and other elementary–school students. Thus, after seventeen years of legal maneuvers and lengthy delays, a district court judge finally decided that the time had come for Richmond to eliminate once and for all the remaining vestiges of Jim Crow education. Richmond's passive resistance, though not yet dead, had received a staggering blow.[37]

Ever since *Brown* II in May 1955, Richmond's school board, like other school districts throughout the South, had interpreted "all deliberate speed" to mean "every conceivable delay." As soon as one legalistic ploy was overturned by the federal courts, it was immediately replaced by another, which, if it were to be effective, had to be more inventive than its predecessor. For five years "freedom of choice" served its purpose well. Yet eventually it too was finally exposed for what it was—a carefully crafted subterfuge designed primarily to preserve segregation under the pretense of voluntary choice. Beset by a myriad of difficulties, the vast majority of Richmond's black children remained trapped in segregated schools. For these black children and their parents, it was beginning to appear that school desegregation—despite judicial pronouncements to the contrary— was but a mirage, reappearing periodically only to vanish when it seemed to be within reach. But would busing succeed where all other desegregation plans had failed? For even the most proficient odds makers, this one seemed too close to call.

FOUR

Eye of the Storm:
The Busing Experiment, 1971-73

I ordered busing for the city because I honestly believed that, under the circumstances, it was the only way to have a thoroughly integrated system. I did what I did not only because it was the law, but because it was right.

—Judge Robert R. Merhige (U.S. District Court for Eastern District of Virginia)

The Supreme Court's decision in *Swann v. Charlotte–Mecklenburg* was a watershed in school–desegregation judicial decision making. It was the clearest indication so far that the federal judiciary was now willing to demand real school desegregation, blocked by local filibustering for nearly two decades. In many ways, *Swann* represented the fulfillment of *Brown*. Coming seventeen years after the Supreme Court's landmark decision, *Swann* sought to address the question of segregated assignments in the public schools once and for all. Although its predecessor and companion *Green* had laid much of the groundwork three years earlier by abolishing "freedom of choice," *Swann* was by far the Court's most explicit and unequivocal statement against school segregation. Unlike *Brown*, *Swann* was not shrouded in ambiguity, and its language was plain and unmistakable. School segregation was wrong and had to end, and seventeen years of foot–dragging had proven that the courts could no longer rely on local officials to eliminate the dual school system. Segregation and racial prejudice had been a part of the American landscape for too long, and neither whites nor blacks could be expected to initiate full-scale desegregation in the absence of an affirmative judicial mandate. *Swann* was that mandate, one that signaled the demise of tokenism and the beginning of a revolution that would have implications reaching far beyond the classroom.

Swann was upheld by the Supreme Court on April 21, 1971, just two weeks after Judge Merhige ordered crosstown busing for Richmond. Writing for the unanimous Court, Chief Justice Warren Burger said that school districts had an affirmative duty to use all available tools, including free transportation, to end school segregation once and for all. In what amounted to a major setback for the proponents of the neighborhood school concept, the Court said, "we find no basis for holding that the local school authorities may not be required to employ bus transportation as one tool of school desegregation. Desegregation plans cannot be limited to the walk-in school." The Court continued:

> All things being equal, with no history of discrimination, it might well be desirable to assign pupils to schools nearest their homes. But all things are not equal in a system that has been deliberately constructed and maintained to enforce racial segregation. The remedy for such segregation may be administratively awkward, inconvenient, and even bizarre in some situations and may impose burdens on some; but all awkwardness and inconvenience cannot be avoided in the interim period when remedial adjustments are being made to eliminate the dual school systems.[1]

Now that the Supreme Court had affirmed Merhige's busing decree, Richmond's school board and city officials began to awaken to the new reality that their policy of passive resistance had run its course, and that their only alternative at this point was to make a good–faith effort to comply with Judge Merhige's ruling. It had taken seventeen years to do so, but the ambiguity of "all deliberate speed" had at long last been clarified, and further delays would no longer be tolerated.

Under Merhige's busing plan approximately 21,000 public–school pupils were bused during the 1971–72 school year. To accommodate the additional passengers, the vast majority of whom would now be drawn from the elementary schools, the city was required to purchase at least sixteen new buses for secondary schools at a cost of $120,000 and at least forty buses for elementary schools at $300,000. First-year operating costs were estimated at $97,000. Merhige acknowledged that his proposed plan would be expensive, but noted that "the expense of preparing for the final desegregation of Richmond's schools as current law requires is indeed a minimal price to pay for the assurance that, whatever binding constitutional interpretations intervene, the rights of all citizens . . . will be protected."[2]

City officials were compelled to purchase fifty-six additional school buses, but Richmond's white schoolchildren could not be compelled to ride them. In a meeting at Stratford Hills United Methodist Church the day after Merhige announced his busing plan, nearly two hundred parents and area residents stated their desire to return to freedom of choice. Infuriated by the city's busing plan, almost half of the group indicated that they would be willing to keep their children at home in protest. Several of those present urged parents to contact their elected federal and state representatives and ask them to take steps to remove those officials who "do not meet the needs and wishes of the people." Some even suggested that a constitutional amendment might be needed to curb the excesses of federal judicial power.[3]

The Supreme Court's affirmation of Merhige's busing order did little to blunt the determination of Richmond's antibusing forces, who were adamant that their children would not be bused. Further, demographics made it highly unlikely that court-ordered busing would succeed. Just beyond the city limits lay Henrico and Chesterfield counties, both of which had overwhelmingly white school systems. Some white Richmonders who could afford the additional expense evaded busing, either by sending their children to private schools within the city or by leaving Richmond altogether. To make matters worse, the views expressed by Richmond's two conservative daily newspapers—which frequently printed articles and letters citing the alleged genetic inferiority and immorality of blacks—greatly strengthened the attitudes already held by many Richmond whites.[4] Busing had clearly become the new symbol of the federal government's encroachment upon state's rights, and the opponents of integration, many of whom now considered it impolitic to be openly racially prejudiced, were quick to adopt busing as the new focus of their animosity.

Richmond's blacks were more receptive to busing, primarily because they viewed it as one way of providing their children with a better education and because they remembered when they had been bused to maintain segregation. Henry L. Marsh III remembered having had to ride in the back of a city bus every day to attend an all-black school, despite the fact that he lived much closer to one of the best white schools in the city. "I was bused," Marsh said with a grin. "I rode the city bus right past John Marshall [all-white] to go to Maggie Walker [all-black]. It was obvious that the schools were not equal, and we were all aware of it. For example, several foreign languages were not available to us at Maggie Walker, and we had to take physics in the back of a chemistry class." Former student and teacher George L. Jones had similar recollections. He explained that many of the black schools were so small that the children had to change classes by going from one school to another, which in many instances meant walking several blocks in the pouring rain and freezing temperatures. "During those days blacks would have been happy to see a school bus. But since so many blacks simply couldn't afford to ride the city buses, we had no choice but to keep on walking."[5]

Some citizens' groups, while perhaps not in total agreement with Merhige's busing decision, were strongly committed to public education and worked to ensure that the busing issue did not destroy the city's school system. One such group was Citizens for Excellent Public Schools, a biracial coalition of parents and interested residents that was officially organized in November 1970. CEPS, which refused to take a public stance on busing, maintained that its primary objective was to convince white and black parents that they had a common interest in preserving the public schools and that the needs of the children should be paramount, no matter how the parents themselves may have felt about busing. The group, hoping to canvass support for the public schools, held forums, took out newspaper advertisements, circulated memoranda, and frequently solicited the influence of some of the city's more prominent citizens. Despite the dedication of many of the group's members, such as A. Jarrell Raper, a white physician, and Melvin Law, a black chemist, CEPS faced an uphill struggle from the outset, and disillusionment began to set in as it became evident that despite the group's honorable intentions, support for public education was on the decline.[6]

Ironically, it was Virginia's governor, Linwood Holton, who performed one of the most courageous acts during the busing crisis. On the first day of classes of the 1970–71 school year, Holton personally escorted his thirteen-year-old daughter Tayloe to predominantly black John F. Kennedy High School, the school to which she had been assigned under the court's busing plan. Meanwhile, Mrs. Holton was taking their other two children, Ann, twelve, and Woody, eleven, to Mosby Middle School, where they were the only whites in their respective classrooms. Many Virginians were shocked, but many others were impressed by the Holtons' act of courage and good faith, especially when it was learned that the governor's mansion is on state—not city—property, and thus the Holton children were technically exempt from the city desegregation plan.[7]

For moral as well as political reasons, Linwood Holton was determined to play a major role in leading Virginia down a more progressive path in race relations. A native of Roanoke, Virginia, Holton attended Washington and Lee University in Lexington, Virginia. After graduating from Harvard Law School, he returned to Roanoke to practice law and to help build the Republican party so that the state could have what he termed "two-party democracy." His efforts to build a strong Republican party reached fruition in 1969, when he was elected Virginia's governor, becoming the first Republican since Reconstruction to hold that office. Now that he held the state's top post, Holton proceeded to articulate a position that supported equal opportunity for all of Virginia's citizens. That pronouncement alone was sufficient to earn him a special place in Virginia's history.[8]

It soon became apparent that Holton's political orientation differed radically from that of those individuals who had occupied the governor's mansion before him. A moderate who had opposed Virginia's massive resistance from the beginning, Holton wanted to eradicate the vestiges of racial discrimination. His inaugural address rang with egalitarian phrases that indicated a strong commitment to equal rights. He spoke of Virginia as being a "model of race relations" and a state whose aristocracy would be determined only by ability. The one phrase that perhaps best captured the essence of Holton's tenure as governor—"the age of defiance is past"— clearly set him apart from most other Virginia politicians of the day. In a 1987 interview, Holton spoke candidly and passionately about his personal convictions regarding integration and his decision to comply with Merhige's busing order:

> Integration was morally right. In my inaugural address I had urged Virginians to recognize that the age of defiance had passed, and here was a ready-made situation where I could walk onto the front page of the New York *Times* and say to the whole world, "You see, we're law–abiding here in Virginia, and this is right." No one could have had a better political opportunity than my family had that day to do something that was right, to show that it could be done without violence, and to show that people would support it because it was right. It was a thrill of a lifetime for me to have that opportunity.
>
> I wanted to make a plain demonstration that this governor and this commonwealth was a law-abiding group and that we could comply with the orders of the courts. And I could see that picture of my daughter and me [entering predominantly black John F. Kennedy High School] juxtaposed against the Ross Barnetts and the George Wallaces saying, "You ain't a coming." Makes me feel pretty good.[9]

Despite Holton's efforts to move Virginia forward on racial matters, many white Virginians were still too deeply rooted in the psychology of massive resistance, and they used the voting booths to express their dissatisfaction with Holton's progressivism. Candidates who had earlier considered the governor's endorsement a blessing soon learned that it was a curse instead, as Holton-supported candidates were soundly defeated in the next two statewide elections. Yet despite the political fallout, Holton remained committed to school desegregation, although his support for busing began to wane.

Holton's public stance on school integration certainly did not endear him to Virginia conservatives, and there can be little doubt that his support of school desegregation's end, coming at a time when the nation was bitterly divided over its means, ended his political career. Holton believes (as do many political observers) that his position on school desegregation probably cost him a seat in the United States Senate. And while admitting that a seat in the Senate would certainly have been desirable, Holton maintains unapologetically that there is nothing he could have accomplished as a U.S. senator that could possibly have brought him more distinction or personal satisfaction than the controversial decisions he made as Virginia's governor:

> Although I respect the United States Senate as a great institution, I know now

that I would be out of place in it. I have no regrets whatsoever about the decisions I made concerning school integration—even if it cost me the Senate. If I had a chance to do it all over again, I would do it stronger if I could figure out a way how.

A career in the Senate, no matter how distinguished it might have been, could not possibly have brought me the gratification I received from just one comment made by an old black man while I was touring Southside Virginia. Something made me speak to that old gentleman. He was bowed, and appeared to be really old, certainly in his eighties. He indicated that he wanted to say something to me, so I leaned over to hear what he wanted to tell me. And in a soft, dignified voice that I will never forget he said, "first governor of all the people." Nobody has ever topped that one.[10]

In a recent article on Holton, Richmond *Times-Dispatch* reporter William Ruberry perhaps summed it up best: "Perhaps if he had been more of a politician, had stroked those who needed stroking, had compromised instead of standing firm, he would have won a 1978 Senate nomination. . . But a rise to greater personal prominence might have come at the expense of his most striking and momentous achievement: breaking sharply with the past to usher in a new era for race relations in the heart of the old Confederacy. A bright star once considered destined for lofty political heights, Holton was brought down by the very events that secured his place in history."[11]

As governor of Virginia during the years of the busing crisis, Holton's primary concern was "to keep the schools open and make sure they survived." Only then, he believed, could the legacy of segregation and massive resistance truly be eradicated. In many respects he succeeded, displaying a style of leadership that forced supporters and detractors alike to take an introspective glance at their own prejudices. Still, his actions alone could not prevent many of Richmond's whites from abandoning the city, and their gradual but steady exodus to the neighboring lily-white suburbs continued unabated.

The exodus of whites from the core cities to the suburban counties has been referred to as white flight, a phenomenon that actually began in the late 1940s. At that time, many people were just beginning to recover from the hard times that had accompanied the depression of the 1930s. Further, because many Americans had been preoccupied with the Second World War, few gave serious thought to the prospect of buying new homes. But as soon as they had fully rebounded from these two major crises, urban dwellers began leaving the crowded conditions of the cities in search of additional living space (readily available in the counties) that would accommodate their growing families.

It is obvious, then, that whites left the cities for a variety of reasons, and Richmond was not the only city to experience this phenomenon. Yet, it seems equally obvious that opposition to busing prompted a good many whites to abandon Richmond in favor of the overwhelmingly white suburbs. It is impossible to determine with any reasonable degree of certainty the actual number of whites who left Richmond in protest over busing, but that some white families left specifically for that reason cannot be denied, especially when suburban relocation is viewed within the context of the city's history of racial intolerance. Many whites who were only slightly offended when their older children were bused became enraged at the mere suggestion that their younger children be bused into black neighborhoods. Of still greater concern to many white parents was that their young, impressionable children would now be taught by black teachers and supervised by black administrators. No doubt, many viewed this urban exodus as an extension of passive resistance to school desegregation, the only difference being that this strategy was pursued as a long-term solution rather than a short-term delay.

In an article published in 1975, two University of Richmond professors noted the extent to which white flight contributed to resegregation within the Richmond metropolitan area:

> While the overall population figures have decreased in Richmond and increased in the counties, the percentage of blacks in each jurisdiction has changed inversely. Containment of blacks within Richmond, rather than significant black immigration, accounted for the increased percentage of blacks in the city. Although black immigration exceeds emigration, and the black birth rate since 1956 has been higher than the white birth rate, *the primary factor responsible for the increased proportion of blacks is continual white emigration.*[12]

Real estate brokers moved in quickly to exploit the fears of white homeowners concerned that property values would depreciate as the number of black city residents increased. In the 1968 Sartain Report, a study of resegregation in the northside schools, a team of urban specialists discovered that a concerted "block busting" campaign had been under way in Richmond for quite some time, with black and white real estate brokers working in happy cooperation with each other. The following is a description of a typical block busting operation:

> A white realtor finds a white couple who is willing to sell to a Negro. The couple is put into contact with the Negro broker who sells the home to a Negro couple, at a higher price than a white would pay, and sends one half commission to the white realtor. Surrounding home owners are put in touch with the Negro broker, and so goes the block. Out to the country and a new suburban home and school goes the white.
>
> Another pressure, but from a different direction, has been the construction of many white suburban developments. The realtors must fill up these new projects and they do this by "opening" new blocks to Negroes. This pressures the whites in the area to move out of the city into the suburban areas. . . .

One [white] family reported that hardly a month goes by without a real estate man calling, trying to get them to offer their house for sale to Negroes.[13]

The demographic configuration of the Richmond metropolitan area was changing rapidly, and according to several interested observers, the change hardly went unnoticed. Marsha Vandervall, a black high school student at that time, recalled how quickly her neighborhood changed from overwhelmingly white to overwhelmingly black:

My neighborhood [the Carillon Area in Richmond's West End] was about 90 percent white in 1971. And it was only within about two years after my family moved there that the ratio changed—almost overnight. We could actually see the neighborhood changing right before our eyes. The "For Sale" signs would go up daily, and you could literally see the blacks moving in and the whites moving out. When my family first moved into that neighborhood, one of the blocks had ten houses on one side of the street, and there were six white families living in them. Within a year or so, there was only one white family left on that block.[14]

Former school board member Virginia Crockford recalled that a similar conversion was well under way in her neighborhood, as indeed it was throughout much of the city, at about the same time:

White families left in droves. Our PTAs dwindled to almost nothing, and many families moved out. I get real depressed when I think about it. A number of parents sent their children to live with relatives so they wouldn't have to attend schools in Richmond. A number of people I heard of sent the children to live with grandparents—some as far away as West Virginia. And others, who claimed they didn't believe in busing, sent their children to the [private] academies, and they bused them much further than they would have been bused in the city. Some of the children in these academies were riding about an hour a day, and I think it's a crime to do that to a child.[15]

Though few would admit it, massive integration, not extensive transportation, was the overriding concern of many whites during the early years of school desegregation. Although it is certain that some of these concerns were born out of racial prejudice, much of the anxiety and trepidation experienced by both blacks and whites resulted from a natural fear of the unknown. For integration meant much more than just race mixing; it involved the bringing together of two separate and distinct cultures, neither of which had a wholly enlightened view of the other. "Parents were quick to react," remembered Virginia Crockford. "Some of the phone calls I got [while serving on the school board] wouldn't have been made if the two students involved had been white. A lot of white people had the fear that if their children went to school with blacks that they were going to get robbed. I had a lot of calls about that."[16]

Then, of course, there was always the ever-present fear that racial tensions would inevitably lead to a violent confrontation whenever the two races came together. Because administrators made a concerted effort to minimize the interaction between blacks and whites, they created an atmosphere devoid of interracial cooperation and detrimental to the smooth operation of the public schools. George H. Johnson, a black former teacher and athletic director at Maggie Walker and John Marshall high schools, remembered that when desegregation first began, the administration considered it a calculated risk to hold extra-curricular activities at night; hence, such events were usually held in the afternoon. "These afternoon events attracted few students and virtually no parents, since they were all working. But then that was the general idea." Johnson admitted that at first there were some parking–lot incidents between groups of blacks and whites, but he pointed out that in most instances the troublemakers were local residents who had no children in the public schools and no interest whatsoever in trying to make desegregation work. "I think that many of them thought of integration as some kind of social experiment, and they wanted it to fail. Some seemed willing to do almost anything to contribute to its demise." No matter who was involved, or whatever their motivations, school desegregation could not proceed peacefully as long as the city was torn apart by racial strife.[17]

Just as some white parents and students abandoned the city and its schools, so too did some of the white teachers. Some of the older white teachers, unwilling to teach in a predominantly black system, took early retirement. Others sought jobs in private schools or in the counties. For those whites who remained, either out of a sense of missionary zeal or because they lacked other options, frustration at times exploded into uncontrolled rage. One white teacher, a former president of the Richmond Education Association, expressed the sentiment of many of her colleagues in an emotional outburst at a school board meeting: "There isn't one of us who isn't physically spent, there isn't a one of us who wouldn't quit and move and teach or work somewhere else if we could find a job. It is humiliating. I'm giving you my gut feeling because I feel that somebody has to stand up and be counted." The schools had become desegregation's major battleground, and the teachers, both black and white, were caught in the middle.[18]

Less than six months after Merhige's busing decree, the black plaintiffs were back in the courts again, this time demanding that the city's school system be merged with those of Henrico and Chesterfield counties. The plaintiffs' attorneys argued that the state had an obligation to eliminate all vestiges of past discrimination by creating a unitary school system that was no longer racially identifiable; this, they maintained, could never happen as long as the city schools remained predominantly black and the county schools overwhelmingly white. Under the proposed merger, Richmond's public schools, a 43,000–pupil system that was 70 percent black, would be consolidated with those of Henrico and Chesterfield, each of which had a student population exceeding 90 percent white. The result would be a single 104,000–pupil unit that would be one-third black.[19]

Reaction to the proposed merger was swift. Virginia's attorney general's office immediately issued a statement that it would oppose such a move. One member of Henrico's board of supervisors urged the county to withdraw from the Richmond Regional Planning District Commission and to void all water and sewer contracts with the city. Local parent–teacher associations—along with newly formed neighborhood groups such as the all-white Citizens against Busing, the West End Concerned Parents and Friends, and the West End Parents Opposed to Busing—passed resolutions denouncing busing and advocating a return to neighborhood schools and freedom of choice. Some organizations, such as Citizens for Excellent Public Schools, took no position at all, while others, such as the NAACP and the Southern Christian Leadership Conference, strongly supported the merger.[20]

When Merhige first suggested the possibility of a merger in 1969, many wondered if such a bold and far-reaching decision would be upheld by the United States Supreme Court, which, with the 1971 appointments of moderate conservative Lewis F. Powell and staunch conservative William R. Rehnquist, was not nearly as liberal as the Warren Court had been twenty years earlier. Although the Burger Court had unanimously approved busing as a desegregation tool in 1971, many believed that the Court would stop short of ordering metropolitan consolidation, because doing so would effectively shut off the last remaining escape hatch for those whites wishing to avoid massive integration without abandoning the public schools. This highly controversial issue, which had been hanging in legal limbo for three years, had finally reached the courts, and metropolitan school districts throughout the entire country anxiously awaited the outcome.

Charles Cox, education reporter for the Richmond *Times–Dispatch* from 1969 to 1987, recalled that the merger trial created an atmosphere of mass hysteria for many white Richmonders, and in some instances proved to be the last straw for those who were on the brink of abandoning the public schools. During the course of the six–week–long trial, Cox wrote a series of articles that outlined the respective arguments of the city plaintiffs and the county defendants. Cox recalled that one particular article—in which he suggested that the counties might be losing their battle against metropolitan consolidation—incited a rash of protest meetings in the counties, resulted in numerous threats on his life, and produced perhaps the angriest response he ever received as a reporter. According to Cox, an irate woman (whom he assumed to be white) called him on the telephone and shouted, "That stuff you wrote this morning, that did it. My house is going on the market today, and I'm going to get the hell out of this goddamn city." Such abusive phone calls became so frequent that the newspaper had to change Cox's number and remove his name from all directories. Meanwhile, the number of whites leaving the city increased dramatically. "Some days there were not enough pages in the paper to hold all the housing ads," Cox said. "It was a diseased time."[21]

During the trial, which began in September 1971, the Richmond School Board (which, although a *defendant* in the school–desegregation cases since the litigation began in 1958, had since filed a cross-motion to become a coplaintiff along with the original black plaintiffs) argued that the metropolitan area had a racially segregated system and that the state had neglected its constitutional obligation to dismantle the system. The school board also emphasized the fact that over the last several decades, even as Richmond got blacker and the counties got whiter, the racial composition of the metropolitan area as a whole remained stable, with blacks accounting for one-third of the total population. Lawyers for the city also cited the counties' refusal to agree to public housing projects for the poor or to allow private contractors to build developments for low-income families. The plaintiffs further maintained that the state had used numerous devices, such as the Pupil Placement Board, tuition grants, and school construction policies to perpetuate classroom segregation.[22]

It is important to note that the plaintiffs' attorneys believed it was sufficient to show that the long-standing segregationist policies and practices of the state and county defendants had contributed to the racial polarization currently existing between the city and the counties. They did not feel it was necessary to establish a direct cause–and–effect relationship between state and county action and increasing metropolitan segregation. Nor did they feel compelled to prove that there existed some kind of conspiracy between the state and counties for the purpose of containing blacks within the inner city. Rather, the plaintiffs sought only to show that in many respects the city and the counties were economically intertwined, and that the impenetrable political demarcations only frustrated school desegregation.

The long-awaited decision was rendered on January 10, 1972. In a 325-page opinion Judge Merhige agreed with the plaintiffs and ordered the merger. The significance of the decision, as well as Merhige's rationale, warrants a substantial quotation:

> Powers enjoyed by the State Board and State Superintendent before and after 1954 have been exercised openly and intentionally to frustrate the desegregation of the three school divisions of the metropolitan area and others throughout the state. The known and foreseeable impact of the manner in which school construction programs were administered, including site selection, choice of school capacity, and quality of facilities, has been to perpetuate the

dual system in each school division. The approval process has been buttressed in this by the powers of the purse, liberally used. The foreseen result has been the continuation of separate and racially identifiable schools, administered by members of a single race, staffed by teachers of a single race, housing pupils of a single race.

School authorities may not constitutionally arrange an attendance zone system which serves only to reproduce in school facilities the prevalent pattern of housing segregation, be it publicly or privately endorsed. To do so is only to endorse with official approval the product of private racism. It is tantamount to the reestablishment of the dual system under a new regime and falls well below the affirmative action necessary and required to desegregate a biracial system.

A Board of Education simply cannot permit a segregated situation to come about and then blithely announce that for a Negro student to gain attendance at a given school all he must do is live within the school's attendance area. To rationalize thusly is to be blinded to the realities of adult life with its prejudices and opposition to integrated housing.

The proof here overwhelmingly establishes that the school division lines between Richmond and the counties coincide with no natural obstacles to speak of and do in fact work to confine blacks on a consistent, wholesale basis within the city, where they reside in segregated neighborhoods.

For the reasons stated in the memorandum of the Court dated January 5, 1972 . . . it is adjudged and ordered that [the governing bodies of Henrico, Chesterfield, and Richmond] forthwith, and in no event longer than thirty (30) days of this date, take all steps and perform all acts necessary to create a single school division composed of the Counties of Chesterfield and Henrico and the City of Richmond.[23]

Judge Merhige's decision sent shock waves throughout the entire metropolitan area. As expected, both counties were outraged and vowed to appeal. A nearly three-hour session of the Chesterfield School Board on January 10 resulted in a statement calling the merger "detrimental to the welfare" of schoolchildren in all three areas. Supervisor Irwin G. Horner called the decision "personal opinions disguised as law." He considered it "outrageous" that the counties should be forced to help solve Richmond's desegregation problems. "If the ruling sticks, this will be the end of the public schools as we know them. They'll become a black public school system and the private schools will be white. We have to rely upon upper courts' reasoning whether they will place integration over education."[24]

County residents were livid. At the first of a series of neighborhood rallies it was proposed that the county residents boycott all city-owned facilities and city-sponsored events, such as concerts, lectures, and sporting events. The parent-teacher associations of both counties, perhaps angrier than any other organized group, adopted resolutions opposing the merger, and many of the teachers threatened to resign if the merger was upheld by the higher courts. Hundreds of students took to the streets, many of them waving antibusing placards. One antibusing group took out a full–page ad in the Richmond *News Leader*. The announcement featured the picture of a schoolhouse and a school bus, the caption below it reading, "This School Bus should take your child to an education . . . not away from it." The culmination of the protest came one week after Merhige's decision, when several thousand county residents, riding in a 3,261-car motorcade that traveled the 108 miles between Richmond and Washington, D.C., made a symbolic trek to Capitol Hill to denounce the ruling. One Henrico County resident assessed the mood of the protesters: "This is middle-class America speaking out. My five-year-old cried when I left this morning, but I told [her] I had to go because it might mean where you go to school. I was a member of the silent majority, until today."[25]

Merhige's consolidation decree was received with mixed emotions in Richmond. Richmond's Mayor Thomas Bliley had a restrained and pragmatic view of the opinion. Urging citizens to remain calm, Bliley said: "I'm not surprised at the decision. The District Court ordered cross-busing for the city sixteen months ago, and had the Court ruled against consolidation its original order would have become meaningless in a very short time." Other members of Richmond's city council expressed differing opinions. Henry L. Marsh, the only black member on city council, praised the decision. He called it a "brilliant recital and analysis of the governmental forces and segregationist practices which have operated to contain blacks in segregated schools and segregated housing." James G. Carpenter, a frequent Marsh ally on council, also hailed the decision. Other council members, however, expressed their indignation over what they considered an unwarranted invasion of a federal judge into the private domain of the state and local governments. Nathan J. Forb said that he was "against busing, regardless of the circumstances," if its sole purpose was to create a racial balance. Howard H. Carwile voiced the strongest opposition to Merhige's decision. He called it "the death knell against public education" in the Richmond metropolitan area.[26]

Remaining consistent with past pronouncements on school integration, the city's newspapers offered a scathing indictment of the merger. The following editorial appeared in the Richmond *Times-Dispatch* the day after the decision:

> What many in this community have feared for months has now been con-
> firmed: U.S. District Judge Robert R. Merhige, Jr. is more interested in
> manipulating human attitudes than in promoting excellent public education.
> This he showed by warmly endorsing, in his school consolidation opinion
> yesterday, the pernicious gibberish of those social engineers who argue, in
> effect, that a school system's primary function is to promote racial together-
> ness, not to give children the best possible academic education. Views to the
> contrary the judge dismissed with patent contempt.

Under Judge Merhige's appalling decision, the schools of the city of Richmond and of the counties of Henrico and Chesterfield will be consolidated next fall unless a higher court acts to avert the tragedy. And tragedy is the right word, for if the decision is allowed to stand, the quality of public education in the Richmond area—and eventually throughout the nation—is almost certain to plummet. . . .

Thus, Judge Merhige approved a mixing plan that would make every school in the metropolitan area predominantly white. This would require the busing of 78,000 pupils, 36,000 of whom would be transported to schools far from their neighborhoods. Rather than submit to such a disruptive order, many parents would abandon public schools.[27]

As hostility to the merger intensified, Merhige became a prime target of abuse. He received a barrage of hate mail, obscene phone calls, life insurance policies, and quite a few Fisher Price toy school buses. Threats to his and his family's lives became commonplace, which eventually prompted authorities to station federal marshals at his home. The following note, sent to the U.S. District Court, is typical of some of the threats Judge Merhige received: "Look—You Dirty Bastard, We are sick of you Federal Judges playing God. Your knowledge of the law is zero minus a million— your left-wing ideology aid [sic] the malcontents to bring this country into revolution. It would be a good idea to look under hood of your car before starting it. Think about it. You son of a bitch."[28]

In the face of such vicious personal attacks, Merhige struggled to maintain his composure. "My family and I went through hell," Merhige said in a 1987 interview.

Federal marshals were assigned to protect me and my family for almost two years. I remember that at one time there were eleven of them living on my property, twenty-four hours a day. They went to school with my son, went to the grocery store with my wife, and they went everywhere with me. The marshals were truly afraid for me, although I was always more concerned about my family. My dog was shot. Our guesthouse, where my then seventy-five year old mother-in-law lived, was burned to the ground. Every other week or so we received a cryptic letter warning that our son Mark would never live to see age twenty-one. I was burned in effigy, spat upon, and occasionally insulted by people who would deliberately walk out of restaurants whenever my wife and I entered. At times it got awfully depressing. But I did what I did not only because it was the law, but also because I believed it was right. And for that, I have no regrets. . . .

People didn't understand. They thought they could do things by consensus. They would come to the courthouse by the thousands, waving their signs which read "Impeach Judge Merhige." But I was determined not to let anybody run me off the bench, and during the entire crisis I never had my telephone number changed. I've always believed that discrimination was a very dehumanizing thing, and I take comfort in knowing that I tried to end it.[29]

Merhige concluded that the state's insistence upon separate school systems within the metropolitan area reflected the desire of state and local officials to maintain as great a degree of segregation as possible. The defendants' main line of defense—that the state had established the political boundaries and that they could not be violated—lacked credibility in light of the state's past history. The state tuition–grant system, which was a feature of the massive resistance legislation, had funded the transfer of white children *across* school–district lines to attend schools in other districts that were segregated. Further, Merhige believed that public schools are the responsibility of the state, and that local school boundaries could easily be adjusted to eliminate racial isolation.[30]

Merhige's decision now paved the way for the desegregation of affluent suburban whites with poor urban blacks. But many were quick to criticize Merhige for ordering integration for *their* children while placing his own eleven-year-old son, Mark, in an exclusive private academy. In a nationally televised CBS interview, he defended his position and refused to offer any apologies: "When I'm on the bench I'm a judge, and when I'm at home I'm just a father. Mark attends a private school because that's where I think he can get the best education and I make no apologies for it."[31]

Merhige was frequently perceived as an activist judge who shaped the law to suit his personal preferences; yet his decision to send his own son to a private school appeared inconsistent and contradictory, and perhaps (as his critics charged) hypocritical. Ronald J. Bacigal and Margaret I. Bacigal point out, however, that Merhige "began the process of desegregation as somewhat of a moderate. . . . His initial decisions sought the middle ground, following the lead of other federal judges in attempting to move the South slowly from outright defiance to gradual acceptance of desegregation."[32] Although his cautious approach often subjected him to criticism from both sides, Merhige ultimately pushed school desegregation further than the United States Supreme Court was willing to go.

As expected, the Virginia State Board of Education and Henrico and Chesterfield counties appealed Merhige's decision to the Fourth Circuit Court. During the hearing, which began on April 13, 1972, Philip B. Kurland, law professor at the University of Chicago and special counsel for the defendants, argued that Merhige's consolidation order was without legal precedent and represented "an assertion of naked power by a federal trial court judge" rather than a valid interpretation of Supreme Court desegregation guidelines. Kurland also rejected the theory of "white supremacy in the classroom" that he said was embodied in the federal court order. He described as a "logical fallacy" the idea that "a substantial white majority" in the classroom is necessary if black children are to excel academically. He further maintained that the three school systems were already unitary, and there was no substantial difference between the three systems other than the number of black students enrolled in each. Attorneys for the plaintiffs reiterated their argument that the city schools would remain predominantly black as long as the counties operated separate schools that were overwhelmingly white.[33]

The excitement surrounding Merhige's decision proved to be short-lived. On June 5, 1972, the Fourth Circuit Court of Appeals reviewed Merhige's decision and agreed with the county defendants' argument that the school boundaries in question had not been established to promote segregation, that each of the three systems in the metropolitan area was unitary, and that no two of the systems had conspired between themselves "for the purpose of keeping one unit relatively white by confining blacks to another." In a five-to-one decision the court held that a district judge could not "compel one of the States of the Union to restructure its internal government for the purpose of achieving a racial balance in the assignment of pupils to the public schools." And while acknowledging that the city's schools were getting blacker, the court maintained that there was scant evidence to show that the whites who had left Richmond had relocated in Henrico and Chesterfield. Writing for the majority, Judge J. Braxton Craven continued:

> We think that the root causes of the concentration of blacks in the inner cities of America are simply not known and that the district court could not realistically place on the counties the responsibility for the effect that inner city decay has had on the public schools of Richmond. We are convinced that what little action, if any, the counties may seem to have taken to keep blacks out is slight indeed compared to the myriad reasons, economic, political and social, for the concentration of blacks in Richmond and does not support the conclusion that it has been invidious state action which has resulted in the racial composition of the three school districts. . . . That there has been housing discrimination in all three units is deplorable, but a school case, like a vehicle, can carry only a limited amount of baggage.[34]

One year later, on May 21, 1973, an evenly divided Supreme Court upheld the circuit court's decision. Justice Lewis F. Powell, Jr., declined to participate in the case. The remaining justices split four-to-four and thus left standing the circuit court's opinion.[35] There would be no metropolitan consolidation in Richmond; but this issue, far from being settled with the Supreme Court's split vote, would soon surface again.

The Supreme Court's refusal to uphold Merhige's decision was as much a welcome relief for some as it was a disappointment for others. As much as some may have wanted to deny it, race continued to be a significant factor not only in determining one's position on the issue of metropolitan consolidation but also in the shaping of one's attitudes and perceptions of school desegregation, something that clearly set most blacks and whites apart. Although blacks suppported desegregation for a variety of reasons, their one overriding concern was the quality of education, which many believed would be enhanced by the mere presence of white children in the classroom. They were convinced that whites would always have access to the very best, and that their own children would benefit enormously simply by being a part of that environment.

Whites were equally concerned about the quality of education, but their perspective, influenced by the same set of racist myths and stereotypes that distorted blacks' self-image, led many of them to conclude that integration and quality education were mutually exclusive, and because they already occupied society's "superior" position, their children had nothing to gain by mixing with "inferior" blacks. Furthermore, many whites viewed court-ordered busing and other methods of forced integration as encroachments upon their freedom. They felt that the federal courts, in their haste to compensate blacks for past injustices, were no longer willing to respect what whites considered to be *their* inalienable rights—among them life, liberty, and the right to send their children to whatever schools they wanted. Yet suddenly, with the Nixon administration intensifying its campaign against busing, and an increasingly conservative Supreme Court poised to hear yet another metropolitan consolidation case involving school desegregation in Detroit, all indications were that the liberal wave of the 1960s had now receded. And, as opposition to busing became a more palatable substitute for racism, the neighboring counties of Henrico and Chesterfield (now that they were officially certified white sanctuaries) became all the more attractive to Richmond whites wishing to evade Judge Merhige's 1971 busing decree. Richmond's schools, more than 70 percent black, would have to desegregate alone.

Symbols of the South, the "New" and the "Old." Virginia Governors
Linwood Holton (1970–74), and Mills E. Godwin, Jr.,
(1966–70,1974–78). (Courtesy of the Richmond Newspapers)

These youngsters were among the first to be bused under the city's interim busing plan, which went into effect in August 1970. (Courtesy of the Valentine Museum, Richmond, Virginia)

Governor Holton escorting his thirteen–year–old daughter Tayloe into predominantly black John F. Kennedy High School, the school to which she had been assigned under the city's new busing plan. Major A. P. Tucker of the Capitol Police accompanies the Holtons on the first day of classes, August 31, 1970. (Courtesy of the Richmond Newspapers)

A schoolteacher sits alone in her empty classroom, as all of her white
pupils have refused to attend school as a protest against Judge Merhige's
busing decision. (Courtesy of the Richmond Newspapers)

District Court Judge Robert R. Merhige, Jr., of the Eastern District of Virginia. (Courtesy of the Richmond Newspapers)

Richmond's black triumvirate: Attorneys Oliver W. Hill, Samuel W. Tucker, and Henry L. Marsh, III. (Courtesy of the Richmond Newspapers)

These schoolchildren were part of an antibusing caravan that drove
through various parts of Richmond to show their discontent with busing.
Their pickup truck was one of about thirty–five vehicles that toured with
the mobile demonstration. (Courtesy of the Valentine Museum,
Richmond, Virginia)

Thousands of city and county residents organized rallies and protests to express their opposition to Judge Merhige's busing plan for Richmond and his later decision consolidating Richmond's schools with those of Henrico and Chesterfield counties. (Courtesy of the Richmond Newspapers)

One of many night rallies held to protest busing. Night rallies were popular because most parents worked during the day. (Courtesy of the Valentine Museum, Richmond, Virginia)

These cars were part of the 3,261–car motorcade that traveled from
Richmond to Washington, D.C., organized as a symbolic protest against
Judge Merhige's January 1972 decision to merge Richmond's public
schools with those of Henrico and Chesterfield counties. (Courtesy of the
Valentine Museum, Richmond, Virginia)

FIVE

"Separate but Equal" Revisited: Transformation and Transition, 1974–89

The opposition, by resisting and fighting, delayed school desegregation for such a long period of time that although we won some key battles we might have lost the war. If desegregation had occurred at once, as we tried to get it to happen, I think that we would have retained more whites in the system. By stretching it out over such a long period of time, it enabled whites to leave the system and to gradually move to the counties and get into private schools. The slow pace at which the courts granted us relief permitted our opponents to achieve many of their objectives.

—Henry L. Marsh III (attorney for the plaintiffs, *Bradley v. Richmond School Board*)

Blacks' celebration of the twentieth anniversary of *Brown v. Board of Education* was marred by the Supreme Court's decision in *Milliken v. Bradley*. In the first defeat for desegregation since *Brown*, the Supreme Court ruled that a metropolitan desegregation plan merging Detroit's inner–city schools with fifty-three suburban school districts could not be constitutionally justified.[1] In short, the Court reasoned that since the counties had not created Detroit's segregation problem, they could not be forced to be a part of the solution. White suburbia was "saved," and the bugle of retreat had sounded. The Court apparently was unwilling to shut off the last remaining escape hatch for those whites wishing to avoid desegregation with blacks. Further, liberal critics charged that the Court, increasingly sensitive to the furor over busing, viewed *Milliken* as an opportunity for judicial appeasement. Justice Lewis Powell, who a year earlier had declined to participate in a similar case involving Richmond, this time voted with the majority. In a strong dissent, Justice Thurgood Marshall, who had successfully argued for the plaintiffs in *Brown* twenty years earlier, wrote:

> After 20 years of small, often difficult steps toward the great end [of equal justice under the law], the Court today takes a giant step backwards. . . . Desegregation is not and was never expected to be an easy task. Racial attitudes ingrained in our nation's childhood and adolescence are not quickly thrown aside in its middle years. But just as the inconvenience of some cannot be allowed to stand in the way of the rights of others, so public opposition, no matter how strident, cannot be permitted to divert this Court from the enforcement of the constitutional principles at issue in this case. Today's holding, I fear, is more a reflection of a perceived public mood that we have gone far enough in enforcing the Constitution's guarantee of equal justice than it is the product of neutral principles of law. In the short run, it may seem to be the easier course to allow our great metropolitan areas to be divided up each into two cities—one white, the other black—but it is a course, I predict, our people will ultimately regret.[2]

When the Supreme Court outlawed "separate but equal" in 1954, black Americans had reason to believe that the end of legalized segregation was near. Despite ominous predictions of prolonged resistance, even the most pessimistic supporters of school integration would not have believed that twenty years later school segregation would still be a reality. Yet, by the mid 1970s, the resegregation of Richmond's public schools was well under way. Since the 1970–71 school year, roughly 12,000 white pupils had abandoned the city's schools, and in 1976 Richmond's black enrollment reached 80 percent. And, as in *Milliken,* the Supreme Court in Richmond's metropolitan consolidation case had failed to take into account the extent to which local and state governments had hindered school desegregation by promoting housing segregation, an issue that seemed to be beyond the reach of the law. Clearly many of the city's black residents were disillusioned with the lack of progress that had been made and had all but given up hope that the schools would ever be desegregated. Many were now beginning to accept the cynic's definition of desegregation—the time between the first blacks moving in and the last whites moving out.

The years immediately following the Supreme Court's controversial decision on metropolitan consolidation can best be described as a period of transition and adjustment. Preoccupation with those students who had left the system caused school officials to lose sight of those who remained. Education was still the primary function of a school system and had to be regarded as such; and while a significant number of whites had fled the city's schools, some cultural exchange between the races would still occur, although on a much smaller scale than some had hoped for.

The initial interaction between blacks and whites was fraught with difficulties, primarily because of the inbred fear and mistrust that each had of the other. Both blacks and whites remembered all too well the racial violence that had erupted in the two preceding decades over attempts to desegregate the schools—the image of Central High School in Little Rock still lingered hauntingly in their minds. And while the physical and psychological abuse that black children had suffered in predominantly white schools was perhaps of little concern to white parents at the time, their fears about such episodes heightened considerably when the situation was reversed. For some whites, concern turned to paranoia, and they reacted accordingly. Arnold R. Henderson, Jr., former principal of Maggie Walker and John F. Kennedy high schools, recalls that whites were so paranoid about sending their children to predominantly black schools that some panicked when they learned that black students were taking karate lessons. "One white lady even went so far as to call the superintendent and to suggest that blacks were learning karate so that they could carry out a mass attack against white students," said Henderson. These kinds of reactions, by no means isolated incidents, were typical of the apprehensions and anxieties during the early years of Richmond's black majority.[3]

If parents had trouble getting used to the reality of a black school system, this sudden transformation was even more traumatic for the teachers, many of whom found it difficult to adjust. But within a very short time most of those teachers who decided to stay realized that if desegregation were to proceed smoothly they would have to set a good example for the students. "We didn't impose any rules on the students that the faculty could not abide by," recalled Herman L. Carter, Jr., former teacher and principal at Kennedy High School. "Some ground rules were established, and everybody was expected to comply. We [the administration] made it clear at the outset that we would not tolerate petty personality conflicts that might have stemmed from racial prejudice. If a certain teacher did not like another teacher, then that was a personal problem, and we didn't deal with it. But we made it clear that there had to be a degree of cooperation in order to ensure the successful operation of the program. Everybody had to play his role, and all had to be of one accord."[4]

Conflicts between teacher and student, however, clearly posed a more serious threat to classroom stability, as many believed these confrontations carried a greater potential for violence. Consequently, black teachers were sometimes very cautious about imposing discipline on white students, as they had been so accustomed to doing with black students. White teachers, perhaps to a far greater degree, were reluctant to tell black students to sit down and be quiet, as they had routinely done with whites. After all, most Richmond schools now had a clear black majority, and white teachers and students alike felt the need to tread lightly. Angelo Setien, a white teacher

at Thomas Jefferson High School and former principal of George Wythe
High School, admitted that for a while he and other white teachers were
very careful when dealing with black students. "Sometimes we felt as
though we were walking on eggs," recalled Setien. "Some of the white
teachers were simply afraid to approach black students and ask them to put
out cigarettes. I know that most of our teachers were well-intentioned, but
they often used the wrong words, like 'boy,' which often triggered conflict.
They made mistakes, but they learned from them."[5]

The consensus among most of the black students was that their white
teachers fell neatly into one of two camps: (1) the paternalists, who felt
that they were fulfilling some kind of missionary zeal by teaching black
children, and (2) the bigots, who were indifferent to the plight of black
students, but remained in the city's school system because they lacked other
options. Marsha Vandervall remembered that some of the white teachers
who taught at Kennedy were "cooperative to the point that they were
sickening, because they felt they had to go the extra mile to help these poor
little black ghetto children. Yet, there were others who couldn't have cared
less. Their attitude was one of 'I'm here, I present it—if you catch it, good;
if you don't, it's not my problem.'"[6]

Not surprisingly, there appeared to have been a direct correlation
between the percentage of blacks in a school's population and the anxiety
level of white teachers. As one increased, so too did the other. Some of the
white teachers who had been assigned to schools located in predominantly
black neighborhoods lived in constant fear of being assaulted. For the most
part, they stayed in groups and were careful not to walk the halls alone;
under no circumstances would they stray too far away from the school
building. Though this antisocial behavior was tolerated at first, the administration eventually had to remind teachers that, like it or not, meting out
discipline to recalcitrant students was part of a teacher's responsibility. All
duty assignments—hall duty, cafeteria duty, yard duty, whatever—were to
be equally divided between black and white teachers. And while it was
understood that extremely delicate and personal matters involving students
might, in some instances, be more easily resolved if both teacher and
student were of the same race, it was generally assumed that all teachers
would act in a supervisory capacity over all students, regardless of race. As
one black teacher put it, "white teachers soon learned that they were
expected to go into the restrooms and break up the crap games like everybody else."[7]

In an attempt to minimize contact between blacks and whites and to
eliminate the possibility of unnecessary friction, some schools curtailed
extracurricular activities, especially those customarily held at night. For
some schools, this meant rescheduling athletic events in the afternoon while
adults were working. Social events, like dances, discos, and proms, were

also restricted at some schools but were permitted at others, depending upon whether or not there were enough teachers to serve as chaperones. As a general rule, the heavier the racial imbalance, the fewer restrictions were placed on after-school social events, since the minority group was perceived as being too insignificant to challenge the majority's dominance. But at schools where the numbers were more evenly balanced, racial tensions were sometimes more volatile, and administrators felt that under those circumstances the less interaction between the races the better.[8]

The prevailing fears and anxieties shared by parents, teachers, and administrators during the 1970s appear to have been unfounded. Given the racial climate of the times, most now agree that the students got along about as well as could be expected—clearly no worse than students in other desegregated schools, and decidedly better than many pessimists had predicted. There were arguments and fights, to be sure. But these altercations stemmed mostly from normal playground disputes that usually had nothing to do with race. "Few of the problems that I had to deal with as assistant principal [at Kennedy High School] had racial overtones," said Herman Carter. "Now there were fights—but whenever you get children together, you're going to have fights, no matter what color they are. To the best of my recollection, there were few fights that stemmed from racial tensions; most fights stemmed from the usual things, like 'why did you bump into me,' or 'why did you cut the lunch line,' and so on."[9]

There were certain students, black and white, who, though not always among the brightest and the best, tried to promote interracial harmony. Despite prevailing racial attitudes, some of the students displayed exemplary leadership in their attempts to break down racial barriers. George H. Johnson, a black former coach and athletic director at John Marshall High School, recalls how well black and white students could work together, even in potentially explosive situations:

> The kids themselves got along all right, but there were prevailing racial attitudes throughout various neighborhoods that caused some tension on more than one occasion. One year, we put on our annual production, which was a musical, *West Side Story*. Playing the lead roles were the white daughter of a prominent real estate developer and a black boy. The kids put up placards throughout the city, showing the white girl and black boy together. And to complicate matters, the black boy was actually dating a white girl [not the white girl in the play]. All hell broke loose. Phones rang for days. But the teachers and administrators kept their cool. They felt that if the students were comfortable with it, why should a few bigots be allowed to spoil it. So the decision was made to run the show as planned. And we had packed houses for the first three nights. There were no repercussions whatsoever.[10]

Other teachers remember that the same spirit of interracial cooperation also existed at their schools. Angelo Setien explains:

There were a lot of touchy issues to deal with at Wythe [predominantly white]; how many blacks should be on the cheerleading squad; who would be homecoming queen; the types of music to be played at the prom, and so forth. Sometimes we even ended up with two bands for a dance. There were so many things that distracted from schoolwork. But the students themselves did a better job than the adults.

I never have understood this, but I guess it just goes to show what the students were like. During the first year of integration, our students elected a black to be student body president and a black girl to be homecoming queen. The student population was 80 percent white! So that shows you what youngsters were doing and what they could do without parental influence, acting strictly on their own.[11]

Though there appears to have been a high degree of interracial cooperation among the students, there were times when social custom and an ingrained inclination toward racial solidarity frustrated efforts to tear down all racial barriers. George H. Johnson remembered that the same students who had successfully pulled off the controversial play met with much less success when they tried to integrate the school cafeteria: "One of the problems we faced was segregation during the lunch period. We had three cafeterias—A, B, and C. The teachers ate in B, the blacks ate in C, and the whites ate in A. This was all by choice. A group of black and white students got together and decided to try to integrate the cafeterias. So, for a while, some blacks ate in the white cafeteria, and some whites ate in the black cafeteria. But this lasted only for a few weeks. After that, they all went back to the old way. But at least the effort was made."[12]

Apparently, white and black students had set their own limits, and, therefore, had drawn a clear distinction between extracurricular cooperation and cultural assimilation. While some of them were willing to work together to ensure the successful implementation of the former, neither group wished to embrace the latter. Retaining a unique cultural heritage and racial identity was as important to blacks as it was to whites; but the prearranged social order, in which whites had been consigned to the top of the caste hierarchy and blacks to the bottom, caused many whites to loathe all aspects of black culture. Moreover, white parents feared that the blacker the city's schools became, the more inclined their children would be to acquire manners and values different from and inferior to their own. Assimilation was a two-way process, and, from a white point of view, white children could be as adversely affected as black children were positively affected. It was a "risk" that many white parents were unwilling to take.

In 1976, Richard C. Hunter became the first black superintendent of Richmond's public schools. One of the first problems he had to contend with was the rapid rate at which the schools were becoming resegregated. In 1978, after securing the approval of both the school board and the district court, Hunter implemented a new desegregation plan, "K–5" (kindergarten through grade five), which was designed to make the city schools more attractive to white parents by giving them the option to keep their younger children in neighborhood schools. By eliminating busing for some of the children, Hunter hoped at least to slow the pace at which whites left Richmond. While black parents had the same set of options, those who wanted desegregation had to have *their* children bused into white neighborhoods. Once again, blacks had to bear most of desegregation's burden.[13]

Richmond's black community had mixed emotions about the new desegregation plan. While some praised it as a step in the right direction, others felt that the plan unfairly sheltered white children from busing. For many blacks, this modified busing plan bore a striking resemblance to other desegregation plans of the past under which blacks had always had to take the initiative. Whites could ride school buses as well as blacks, and any desegregation plan that did not distribute the burden of busing equitably would never receive the wholehearted endorsement of the black community. Clearly, many blacks who had welcomed busing a decade earlier were now having second thoughts.

Despite Hunter's efforts, Richmond's schools continued to lose more students every year. Declining enrollments owing to white flight and fewer births meant that there were simply too many schools operating in the city. Many believed that the only practical solution was to close some of the schools, but no one could agree on the selection process to be used in determining which schools would be closed. It was clear, though, that something would have to be done soon, especially at the high–school level, where student losses were particularly acute. Some high schools that had a capacity of nearly 2,000 enrolled fewer than 600.

In early 1978, school administrators began discussing plans that might offer a solution to the city's declining school population. Rather than close any of the high schools, they decided that merger might be a better solution. Despite some initial skepticism, most eventually agreed that merger was perhaps the best way to utilize the various facilities available at all of the schools. The proposed merger, known as Plan G, was adopted by the school board in 1978 and implemented in 1979. Under the plan, the city's seven high schools would become three: Marshall-Walker, Armstrong-Kennedy, and Jefferson-Huguenot-Wythe.

During its years of operation, Plan G remained controversial and unpopular. Critics argued that the plan was a fiscal failure, and that the notion of utilizing all facilities was expounded by administrators too timid to face the reality that eventually some schools would have to be closed. The students, supposedly the intended beneficiaries of the plan, never fully embraced it. Many of them disliked the idea of "their" school being merged with another; nor were they thrilled about the shuttle–bus rides that

were now a part of their school day. They began to feel, as did their
parents, that their school identity had been lost and that their traditions had
been destroyed. These concerns, among others, forced the school board to
dismantle Plan G in 1986. In 1986, six of those high schools went back to
operating as individual units. The seventh, Maggie Walker, was closed as a
regular high school and was later reopened as Community High School, one
of the city's magnet schools.

Events of the 1970s necessitated a serious restructuring of the curriculum in Richmond's public schools, one that could not be accomplished by
new busing plans or school mergers. When whites left the city during the
1970s, they took much of the middle–class tax base with them. The atten-
dant loss of revenue contributed to a general decline in educational standards that ultimately caused many affluent blacks to withdraw their support
from Richmond's public schools. Enrollment figures indicated that the
number of blacks attending Richmond's schools had been declining since
the mid-1970s, while at the same time the number of blacks attending
county schools had been increasing. Henrico and Chesterfield county
schools, both of which had black enrollments of less than 10 percent in
1971, were 26 and 14 percent black, respectively, according to 1987–88
enrollment figures. While the resegregation of the city's schools was
certainly racially motivated to a large degree, discernible class divisions
were becoming readily apparent.

By the early 1980s, Richmond's private schools were beginning to
reflect a similar socioeconomic division. While private education has
always been one of the prerogatives of society's elite, race discrimination,
in all but a few instances, had historically kept this privilege off–limits to
blacks, regardless of their status. But increasing pressure from the federal
government forced these private academies to abandon their racially
restrictive admissions policies if they wanted to retain their tax-exempt
status. Even the remaining segregationist academies, which had been
founded for the express purpose of perpetuating segregation, grudgingly
renounced their discriminatory practices. As a result, these schools began
to recruit minority students, most of whom were drawn from the ranks of
the well-to-do, draining the city of still more of its middle–class base.
Today, practically all of Richmond's private schools have some minority
students, although the numbers remain small. With the affluent of both
races either in the counties' schools or in the city's private schools,
Richmond's public schools are quickly becoming almost as poor as they are
black.[14]

As this new socioeconomic realignment was taking place in the 1970s,
educational standards in the city's schools were declining at an alarming
rate. In almost every category, Richmond's public schools were worse off
each succeeding year than they had been the year before, something which,

to a degree, was expected. "It came as little surprise to me that the quality of education took a turn for the worse in the early 1970s," said superintendent Richard Hunter. "Some decline in academic standards was inevitable during the early years of desegregation. There were simply too many factors working against us. Education was bound to suffer some setbacks because the schools had served as the major battlegrounds for the desegregation issue. Consequently, some losses were expected. It was a sacrifice that had to be made."[15]

Beginning in the late 1970s, however, school officials agreed that certain curriculum revisions were necessary if educational standards were to improve. Because most of the children were now coming from lower–income families, the teachers had to take a different approach in educating them. But more important, school officials had to accept the fact that it would not be as easy educating children from poor families as it had been educating children from affluent ones. Former school superintendent James W. Tyler explained: "Years ago when we were asked about our schools, our response was always favorable. We were eager to single out such schools as John Marshall, Thomas Jefferson, and George Wythe [all-white schools] as being exceptional. We ignored the fact that many of the students attending Mosby [all-black] were unable to read. But today, just as much emphasis is placed on one school as another. It is our larger objective to make sure that all students receive a quality education."[16]

The curriculum revisions (such as a renewed emphasis on the basics, smaller pupil–to–teacher ratios, more teacher incentives, and an array of special programs) have obviously paid some handsome dividends, and few will deny that Richmond's public schools have come a long way in the past ten years. Yet, in terms of overall performance, Richmond's students still score lower than their suburban counterparts, and the gap has not narrowed appreciably in recent years. These disparities, however, are undoubtedly more clearly related to economic factors than to anything else. Richmond school officials concede that the number of students requiring remedial and special–education programs has increased over the years, and they point out that roughly 6,500 city–school pupils, or nearly 25 percent of the enrollment, live in public housing projects, and more than 60 percent of the student population qualify for free lunch. In 1985 Richmond schools spent more than $20 million to pay for programs specifically aimed at disadvantaged children, much more than was spent by Chesterfield or Henrico.[17] Nonetheless, the city's students are still learning. "There is a mechanism in place in terms of accountability," said former Assistant Superintendent Nathaniel Lee. "We have accepted the fact that our enrollment is predominantly black, but they are still students, and they can learn. We've got all the necessary programs in place to guarantee that our children get the best education possible."[18] (See also tables 2 and 3.)

Table 2. An educational and socioeconomic comparison of students in
Richmond, Henrico, and Chesterfield

	Richmond	Henrico	Chesterfield
Enrollment, September 1989	26,900	31,963	42,950
Number of schools	59	51	48
Race			
White	10.5%	70.9%	83.1%
Black	88.3%	25.8%	14.0%
Other	1.2%	3.3%	2.9%
Failure rate (1988–89)	10.5%	4.3%	4.5%
Dropout rate (1988–89)	12.5%	3.4%	4.2%*
Out–of–school suspensions (1988–89)	1,692	3,337	3,043
Expulsions	30	10	6
Students eligible for lunch subsidies	16,063	3,389+	3,187
Students in Chapter One aid program	4,240‡	1,200	1,062
Special education students	2,094	2,839	4,500
Gifted and talented students (1987–88)	10.6%	8.8%	15.3%
Head start students (1988–89)	272	0	118
Per–pupil expenditures (1987–88)	$5,675	$4,039	$4,501
Computers in the classrooms	2,300	2,100	1,546

*1987–88
+Does not include high–school pupils.
‡Of 16,190 eligible.
Sources: Richmond, Henrico, and Chesterfield public school systems; state department of
education.

Table 3. Racial composition of Richmond public schools

School Year	White	Percent	Black	Percent	Total
1950–51	18,037	58.8	12,642	41.2	30,679
1951–52	18,413	58.8	12,915	41.2	31,328
1952–53	19,526	58.9	13,623	41.1	33,149
1953–54	20,052	57.9	14,592	42.1	34,644
1954–55	20,259	56.5	15,598	43.5	35,857
1955–56	19,853	54.7	16,413	45.3	36,266
1956–57	19,522	52.8	17,479	47.2	37,001
1957–58	19,203	50.9	18,530	49.1	37,733
1958–59	19,209	48.9	20,047	51.1	39,256
1959–60	18,518	46.7	21,166	53.3	39,684
1960–61	18,087	44.5	22,599	55.5	40,686
1961–62	17,743	42.7	23,825	57.3	41,568
1962–63	17,641	41.4	24,955	58.6	42,596
1963–64	17,539	40.2	26,092	59.8	43,631
1964–65	16,957	38.3	27,331	61.7	44,288
1965–66	16,571	37.4	27,792	62.6	44,363
1966–67	15,833	35.7	28,529	64.3	44,362
1967–68	14,724	33.7	29,008	66.3	43,732
1968–69	13,624	31.6	29,441	68.4	43,065
1969–70	12,622	29.5	30,097	70.5	42,719
1970–71	17,203*	35.8	30,785	64.2	47,988
1971–72	13,930	30.9	31,101	69.1	45,031
1972–73	13,078	29.8	30,747	70.2	43,825
1973–74	10,945	26.7	30,015	73.3	40,960
1974–75	9,421	23.9	30,037	76.1	39,458
1975–76	8,211	21.5	30,007	78.5	38,218
1976–77	7,273	19.7	29,693	80.3	36,966
1977–78	6,486	18.3	28,926	81.7	35,412
1978–79	5,842	17.1	28,339	82.9	34,181
1979–80	5,303	16.3	27,274	83.7	32,577
1980–81	4,929	15.6	26,602	84.4	31,531
1981–82	4,224	13.8	26,309	86.2	30,533
1982–83	4,348	14.3	26,001	85.7	30,349
1983–84	4,183	14.0	25,593	86.0	29,776
1984–85	4,022	13.6	25,605	86.4	29,626
1985–86	3,946	13.5	25,214	86.5	29,160
1986–87	3,726	13.0	24,933	87.0	28,659

*Reflects an increase of 5,000 white students due to Richmond's annexation of twenty-three square miles of Chesterfield County.

For almost twenty years Richmond's school officials have been experimenting with magnet schools, a concept that has attracted increasing attention in recent years. Magnet schools (which at times have also been called by a variety of other names, including open, experimental, ungraded, and model schools) are viewed by some as the key to revitalizing the city's public–school system. Some even hope that these schools, with their college–preparatory orientation, will eventually lure some whites back into the system, something that critics dismiss as wishful thinking. And while magnet schools have had their successes, many people are quick to point out that these schools should not be seen as a panacea for all that is ailing the city's school system, and that the turnaround is not likely to happen overnight.

Since these experimental programs first began in the 1970s (the first ones having been started at John B. Cary Elementary School, Bellevue Elementary School, and the Northside Middle School), there has been the hope that such programs would provide students with a degree of independence that would be helpful later on in college. In some of the programs, classes are scattered all over the city, with some being held in museums, public libraries, university classrooms and laboratories, business establishments, and government agencies. Despite the diversity and flexibility, the curriculum is demanding. The students—some of whom take their upper-level courses in classes at Virginia Commonwealth University, the University of Richmond, and Virginia Union University—acknowledge that there is tremendous pressure to succeed. This hard work apparently has paid off, as some of the city's magnet schools consistently attract Ivy League recruiters. Richmond's Community High School, in operation since 1977 and presently housed in the Maggie Walker building, has been referred to by some as "the jewel in the city's school system crown," and is a good example of what magnet schools can accomplish. In its class of 1989–90, nineteen out of the school's forty-one seniors received National Merit or national achievement commendations, and overall, the school has a 99 percent college acceptance rate. Of 193 pupils in 1989-90, 70 percent were black, 25 percent white, 4 percent Asian, and 1 percent Hispanic. About one-fourth of the students would be defined as "at risk"--pupils unlikely to finish high school elsewhere.[19]

Dr. Albert Jones, superintendent of schools since July 1, 1989, has been one of the strongest supporters of magnet schools, and is eager to expand the program by adding more such schools to the system. "I want to expand, duplicate, clone Community High," says Dr. Jones. "We are not talking about anything revolutionary. We're talking about how do we package, develop and deliver to students what we have. There are no surprises. We're talking about blending subjects and presenting them differently to students." A forty-five member task force recommended that it would be best to proceed slowly at first, and then allow the program to expand as public awareness and interest increase. Three new magnet schools were scheduled to open in the fall of 1990: a math, science, and computer-based technology program at John F. Kennedy High School, a visual and performing arts program at George Wythe High School, and a government and international relations program at Thomas Jefferson High School, which is set to become a governor's school. (A governor's school enrolls gifted students from a specific region of the state.)[20]

Dr. Jones contends that as the programs develop, interest will grow, and that soon "the effectiveness will be the proof of the pudding and that will be the major way to recruit students." He is also careful to point out that these programs were not designed to be used as "a carrot for desegregation." When asked if magnet schools will improve academic achievement and raise test scores, he said that standardized test scores are not necessarily the best way to evaluate an urban school system: "We are saving hundreds of students who would normally drop out of schools. It's a secret that needs to be exposed. If you save a student from the streets, from incarceration, reduce the number of pregnancies, teach people to read, get them jobs, these are all kinds of results that don't show up on test scores, but the types of things an urban school system needs to do. . . . The key is what do you do with what you have."[21]

Not everyone shares the superintendent's enthusiasm. One teacher, a thirty-year veteran, compares magnet schools to "putting a new dress on a country girl." Others maintain that such programs are not new, and that despite claims to the contrary, enticing white students to return to the system is indeed one of the underlying motives. These criticisms aside, perhaps the most frequently made argument against magnet schools is that they have been portrayed as a magic solution for all the school system's woes when they clearly do not work for all students. Officials say that students tend to do better in magnet schools because they *want* to be there—their enrollment is strictly voluntary. And while some students have thrived in this kind of setting, others have perished, primarily because of the lack of a more tightly structured curriculum, something that many view as being absolutely vital during the formative years of a student's learning process. Then, of course, there was the ever-present concern that magnet schools—with their college–preparatory orientation—would eventually lead to socioeconomic segregation within the school system. That possibility appears to have been averted, and the issue is raised less and less frequently. Still, the relative merits of magnet schools are constantly being debated, and a consensus is unlikely to emerge any time in the near future.[22]

One of the most intense issues to emerge in the 1980s concerning Richmond's schools has been the question of state funding. Now that the courts have found Richmond's schools to be unitary (or as unitary as they

can be, given the demographic configuration of the metropolitan area) and
that further desegregation with the neighboring counties is neither likely nor
warranted, Richmond's school officials contend that the state has a financial obligation to help eradicate the remaining vestiges of segregation;
therefore, the state should appropriate additional funds to the city's school
system to enable it to achieve parity with its suburban counterparts. In
1986, Richmond's school board, along with various parents, filed a lawsuit
against the state of Virginia seeking $48 million for an extensive remedial
program to eliminate what the school board said was lingering vestiges of
past state-mandated racial segregation.[23] The school board claimed that
Richmond's students continue to suffer from the effects of past discrimination, and that despite recent improvements, "there continues to be a
significant gap between what Richmond students achieve and what students
achieve elsewhere in the state," which is primarily due to the "clear
message" that the state sent its citizens for two hundred years—that whites
and blacks were not to mix. The state countered by arguing that Richmond
received more money per student from the state than the state average and
that it received more than the surrounding counties. Recent progress by
city students "has been profound," the state's attorneys argued, and "not
one single child is forced to wear a badge of inferiority" because he is
enrolled in the city's schools.[24] On July 10, 1986, Judge Merhige dismissed
the suit (and also relinquished his jurisdiction over the Richmond Public
School system), saying that he could find no evidence of lingering discrimination that could be blamed on the state, and even if that were the case, the
state's disproportionately large contribution to Richmond's schools satisfied
any further obligation. "Although the Court feels that one of the reasons for
the high poverty rate in Richmond is the inferior education that was
provided to blacks under the former dual school system," Merhige wrote,
"it is not within the Court's power to remedy either the poverty itself or the
ancillary effects of such poverty."[25] In 1987, the Fourth Circuit Court of
Appeals affirmed Merhige's ruling.[26]

The school board acknowledges that the state has been generous with
the city's schools, but feels it has not been nearly generous enough. A
major bone of contention has been the formula used by the state to determine the amount of funding it should provide. Many point out that the
state's formula takes into account the wealth of the city, which is inflated
by its corporate structure, and does not accurately reflect the economic
status of the public schools' population.[27] Former school board chairman
Melvin Law agrees. "The funding formula is out of date by 100 years,"
and, consequently, "Richmond is considered more wealthy than Chesterfield or Henrico. Equitable funding for Richmond children must be
addressed even though the School Board did not prevail in its litigation of
1985. The issue needs to be revisited."[28]

More money from the state will certainly help Richmond's school system, but it is, after all, only a part of the long-term solution. Educators and administrators agree that perhaps the greatest challenge facing them is to help black children from poor families overcome a crippling legacy of neglect and to convince them that they can learn. It has not been easy for black children to overcome the stigma associated with all-black schools, especially when the academic preparedness of middle–class whites has constantly reminded them of their own educational deficiencies. For some black children, underachievement became a self-fulfilling prophecy; having been told repeatedly that they could not learn, they put forth very little time and effort and therefore did not learn. Educators have spent the last several years trying to reverse that trend by encouraging students to feel good about themselves and to have confidence in their own ability. For Richmond's students, the period of adjustment is over, and they must now capitalize on the support mechanisms that will enable them to get the most out of their learning experience. Effort and initiative will be the only things to stand in their way.

EPILOGUE

A Promise Betrayed:
Thirty-Five Years after Brown

We deal here with the right of all of our children, whatever their race, to
an equal start in life. . . . Those children who have been denied that
right in the past deserve better than to see fences thrown up to deny them
that right in the future. Our nation, I fear, will be ill-served by the
Court's refusal to remedy separate and unequal education, for unless our
children begin to learn together, there is little hope that our people will
ever learn to live together.

—Justice Thurgood Marshall (dissenting opinion,
Milliken v. Bradley)

Judge Robert Merhige believed he was justified in ordering busing for
Richmond in 1970. As he emphasized in his memorandum opinion, a
history of segregation had kept black and white schoolchildren apart;
crosstown busing was one way to bring them together. The United States
Supreme Court had outlawed segregation in *Brown v. Board of Education*,
and had gone a step further in *Green v. New Kent County* by ordering an
end to token desegregation plans that did not work. Busing was necessary,
the Court held in *Swann v. Charlotte-Mecklenburg*, because free public
transportation seemed to be the only way to achieve a unitary school
system. But white backlash was swift; and, while pickets and rallies were
the most visible manifestations of their outrage, the systematic withdrawal
of their children from the city's public schools was by far their strongest
and most unequivocal statement against "forced busing" for integration.
Some whites enrolled in private academies while others sought refuge in

the counties' public school system. And when the Supreme Court had an opportunity to discourage white emigration by ordering a city-county merger, it declined to do so. Hence, in the aftermath of white middle–class flight from the public schools, Richmond developed a new type of dual education—a private school system for the affluent and white, and a public school system for the poor and black.

In April 1986, sixteen years after he ordered busing for Richmond, Merhige approved a neighborhood–school plan that ended it. School buses still operate in the city, but only to provide transportation for those children who live more than a mile and a half from school. Ironically, busing was ended at the behest of the city's majority–black school board (blacks gained control of the board in 1980).[1] Because the school system was 87 percent black, school–board members agreed that crosstown busing did nothing but transport black children from one predominantly black school to another. Because of the scarcity of white children in the city's schools, crosstown busing no longer served the purpose for which it was intended.

In a series of interviews conducted by the Richmond *News Leader* in the fall of 1986, several teachers, administrators, and former students reflected on the events of the past sixteen years and assessed the long-term successes and failures of busing. Though events would indicate that busing is a burden that most Richmond blacks are no longer willing to bear, there was a time when busing for racial balance had the support of most blacks and a few whites because it was the only way to ensure that there would be some equity in education. "Busing put black kids where the resources were," said black former mayor and city councilman Roy A. West, who is also principal of Albert Hill Middle School. "It sent a message to the school board and school administrators that they had a moral obligation to treat children, staff and supplies equally."[2]

William O. Edwards, a black former school–board member, said his youngest child attended city schools before and after busing began. "She told me once she had two kinds of education. We both knew what she meant. She was broadened by the experience." A former principal of what was an all-white high school said "lots of people were unhappy, but I was amazed at the way teachers, parents, and students rallied around to make integration work. It was a traumatic experience, but a rewarding one." Not everyone agreed. Rev. Vernon Gibson, an outspoken opponent of busing in the 1970s, felt that "busing didn't accomplish a thing. It was one of the most haphazard and disastrous things that ever happened to the system." The Reverend Mr. Gibson said that desegregation would have proceeded more smoothly and effectively had people been allowed to make the adjustment gradually and voluntarily.[3]

John V. Moeser, a professor of urban studies and planning at Virginia Commonwealth University, offered a different interpretation of busing.

"Busing didn't fail. Who failed were the large number of white citizens who opted out, who wouldn't give public education a chance." Moeser contends that the "real hypocrisy" of the past sixteen years came from those who claimed they supported integration but were opposed to crosstown busing. Given the alternative of maintaining the status quo, Moeser feels that busing was a positive step. "It took busing, as traumatic as it was, to break out of segregated schools. Under freedom of choice, we still had a system of apartheid. If we had to rely on good will [to end segregation] we'd be waiting one hundred years from now."[4]

Several former students also recalled their experiences during the 1970s and ruminated on the ways in which busing and desegregation had affected their lives. "I felt like a guinea pig, like it was an experiment," remembers John L. Taylor, a black attorney in Richmond who graduated from Armstrong in 1973. But, says Taylor, after a brief period of adjustment, everything returned to normal, the only difference being that now "there was a yellow bus pulling up in front of the school every day." From Taylor's perspective, the most positive aspect of desegregation was that it "gave young black kids an opportunity to destroy some stereotypes built up over the years. I found out that white kids were just normal kids. There were some who made As, and there were some who made Cs, Ds, and Fs. They were just kids, no more, no less. It was the greatest thing in the world, a very enriching experience."[5]

For other students, though, desegregation was laden with tensions and frustrations. Steve Austin, a 1975 graduate of George Wythe, recalls that he usually kept to himself. A white student in a majority black school, Austin dreaded walking the halls or going into the bathrooms because "there was always an element who would ask you for money." He also remembers a lack of school spirit or class unity. He rarely attended the pep rallies because he did not like the kind of music and cheers. "It was mostly what black students liked. There was a definite black style and white style." Then there were the fights—"it seemed like it was whites against blacks, but maybe they stood out more," he said. Ken Martin, another white Wythe graduate, also recalls fights between blacks and whites and being "hit up" for money by black bullies. He said that he and some other white students "had never known any black people. Nobody trusted anybody."[6]

For other white students, the experience was positive. Mark Person, a 1974 graduate of Wythe, said that his parents gave him the option of going to a private school, as many of his friends were doing, but he decided against it. "Personally, I'm glad I went through the experience, from an educational and a human relations standpoint. I was a victim at first. I was mugged as an eighth-grader. If anyone had reason to leave city schools it was me. But I felt a loyalty to stay. I've always believed in my own rights and didn't want to be pushed out of a situation. You get out of something what you put into it." Person went on to participate in baseball, tennis, music, and the Key Club. By the time he reached his senior year, he recalls that "a pretty strong bond" had formed among class members, black and white, despite the tensions of earlier years.[7]

In view of the social and political climate that existed in Richmond during the 1970s, it is a wonder that school desegregation proceeded as well as it did. Two decades earlier, the state's response to the *Brown* decision was to pursue a policy of blatant defiance against the edicts handed down by the Supreme Court, even if it meant closing the public schools. Hence, by the 1970s, abandoning public education was by no means a novel concept for those opposed to integration. More important, though, was that throughout the entire school–desegregation era, white attitudes appear to have changed very little in regard to the degree of race mixing they felt comfortable with. Even during massive resistance, some white moderates expressed a willingness to accept a modicum of desegregation rather than abandon public education altogether. Twenty years later, most whites were still reluctant to move beyond the policy of tokenism.

It may be impossible to single out any one factor as being the primary cause for the persistence of racial intolerance among white Richmonders. Yet, there is a general consensus among blacks and whites alike that the city's two major newspapers were perhaps the greatest obstacle to a smooth transition from segregation to desegregation. Instead of enlightening the Richmond community, the management of both the *News Leader* and the *Times-Dispatch* used their editorial pages to create an atmosphere of mass hysteria and defiance by fanning the flames of emotionalism and racial bigotry, which only served to poison race relations between blacks and whites at a time when understanding and mutual cooperation were desperately needed. By raising the specter of sexual immorality, widespread violence, lower academic standards, and racial amalgamation, the newspapers contributed significantly to the constant erosion of support for the city's schools among the white middle class. The *News Leader*, especially, seized every available opportunity to exploit existing racial tensions by providing front-page coverage of all ugly incidents involving black and white students and by interpreting those incidents as irrefutable evidence that any attempt to bring the two races together in an intimate setting would inevitably result in chaos. Charles Cox, education reporter for the *Times-Dispatch* between 1969 and 1987, offered these observations: "The papers have been blamed, and I personally think justly, for not doing a great deal [to promote school integration]. Had these papers taken a leadership role, had they attempted to encourage people to see that an era had ended, and that we were entering into another one, it might have made things easier. It might not have made all the difference in the world, but it sure would have helped. I hope that I will be seen as being a part of the other side of that."[8]

Virginius Dabney served as the editor of the Richmond *Times-Dispatch* from 1936 to 1969. Dabney was born in University (now Charlottesville), Virginia in 1901; his family, considered to be Virginia aristocracy, included in its ranks numerous planters, lawyers, physicians, and college professors. Dabney was graduated Phi Beta Kappa from the University of Virginia in 1920 and went on to receive his master's degree in 1921. After teaching French for a year at a high school, Dabney became a reporter for the Richmond *News Leader* in 1922, a position he held until 1928, when he joined the editorial staff of the Richmond *Times-Dispatch,* where he would remain for the next forty-one years.[9]

During his distinguished career as a university lecturer, a historian of the Old South, Virginia, and Richmond, and a Pulitzer Prize–winning journalist, Virginius Dabney was regarded by many as one of the South's loudest voices for social change and gentility in race relations. As one writer notes, "the courtly and gracious Dabney was a southerner of liberal instincts, well before such sentiments became fashionable or legally mandated." For example, in 1937, after an NAACP–sponsored antilynching bill was introduced in Congress, Dabney wrote a strongly supportive editorial in the *Times-Dispatch,* and encouraged other southern liberal editors to do the same. In 1938 he called for the immediate repeal of the poll tax (which disfranchised more poor whites than blacks) in Virginia and elsewhere. In 1941 he called upon defense industries to hire blacks and pay them equally with whites. In 1943 Dabney won the praise of the NAACP, the militant black press, and white liberals when he wrote two *Times-Dispatch* editorials urging Virginia to abandon segregation on buses and streetcars. His argument essentially was that trying to get out of each other's way more often than not forced blacks and whites into closer contact with each other than would be the case if they were left to sit wherever they chose. "We white Southerners," Dabney wrote, "can remedy the evident injustices in the treatment of the Negroes, and thereby win their confidence, respect and cooperation, or we can refuse to do anything, and repeat the old nonsense to the effect that 'the problem will solve itself, if people will only stop talking about it.'"[10]

While praised in some quarters, Dabney was denounced in others. Because of white Southern backlash, he was ultimately forced to retreat from some of his earlier positions, such as his support for a federal antilynching bill, and to clarify his position on others, as was evident in his reassuring comment to one worried Virginia woman that he did not propose abolishing segregation anywhere but on common carriers. No doubt it was Dabney's sensitivity to Southern white sensibilities, as well as his own Southern upbringing, that caused him to waver on the issue of total racial equality. Despite his support for some black causes during the 1930s,

1940s, and 1950s, Dabney never favored admitting blacks to white Southern educational institutions under any circumstances, believing that the time was not yet "propitious." His liberalism, it would appear, had its limits, as was true of most other so-called white Southern liberals of his day.[11]

It was this same sense of restrained liberalism that, for the most part, characterized Dabney's tenure as *Times-Dispatch* editor during the years of Richmond's school–desegregation crisis. In a 1989 interview, Dabney reflected on his position as the editor of one of Richmond's two leading newspapers and the extent to which the school–integration issue created sharp conflicts of opinion: "Over the years a lot of people have lumped the two Richmond newspapers together, and gave me credit for being as bad as Kilpatrick. Personally, I was very friendly with Kilpatrick, but I didn't agree with his editorials at all. D. Tennant Bryan, the publisher of both newspapers, decided that he wanted the *News Leader* to be the organ of 'massive resistance.' I thought that closing schools was absolutely ridiculous, and I would have spoken out against it more had I been in a better position." Still, Dabney maintains that he was "never pressured," and generally felt comfortable with the *Times–Dispatch*'s position on school desegregation, although he said he actually "wrote very little about the subject."[12] While it is a fact that the *Times-Dispatch*'s tone was never as strident as the *News Leader*'s, there can be little doubt that Dabney's relative silence on the issue was, in the long run, as much a hindrance to school desegregation as Kilpatrick's incessant diatribe.

More than most other Southern newspaper editors of his day, Virginius Dabney believed in a sense of fair play and used his position to focus attention on many of the injustices that Southern blacks in particular faced daily, and he did so at a time when such views were not popular. For that, he must be given credit. But for whatever reasons, Dabney, by his own admission, "became much more conservative" over the years, a conservatism clearly reflected in his decision not to come out in support of school desegregation.[13] His words of reason and compassion might have made a difference for some who feared the unknown and were desperately seeking courageous moral leadership in a time of confusion and crisis. Dabney failed to seize that opportunity, however, and his acquiesence in maintaining the status quo in segregated public education would indelibly tarnish his progressive image.

It would be impossible—and certainly unfair—to place the blame for desegregation's failure on any one individual or organization, as there were many culprits. In retrospect, it may be easy for some to conclude that because busing was such an abysmal failure—which consequently frustrated school desegregation—it was a terrible mistake, and should never have been attempted. Historians Lino A. Graglia and Raymond Wolters are the foremost proponents of this view.

In *Disaster by Decree: The Supreme Court Decisions on Race and the Schools,* Lino A. Graglia argues:

> On the issue of race and the schools, the Court's enhanced power and status emboldened it to move from *Brown's* prohibition of segregation—the use of racial discrimination to separate the races—to a vastly more ambitious and questionable requirement of integration or "racial balance," the use of racial discrimination to increase racial mixing beyond the mixing that results from prohibition of racial discrimination. . . . What the country needs to understand today in regard to compulsory integration is that, not only has it been imposed by the Supreme Court and not by the Constitution, but it has been imposed by the Court most improperly.[14]

In *The Burden of Brown: Thirty Years of School Desegregation,* Raymond Wolters makes the same argument:

> In preparing this study I have found much that is discouraging about what has happened to public education and to the Constitution. In the *Brown* districts [Clarendon County, South Carolina; Prince Edward County, Virginia; Wilmington, Delaware; Topeka, Kansas; and Washington, D.C.], education has suffered grievously from naively liberal court orders, from the influence of progressive education, and from the defiant and irresponsible behavior of some students. The Constitution has also suffered as judges have arrogated the right to make social policy. Segregation was anachronistic in the middle of the twentieth century, but in a democracy social reform should be undertaken by the people's elected representatives, not by unelected judges. I further believe the Supreme Court erred in policy as well as in prerogative when it moved from color blindness to color consciousness and began to impose remedies that require racial balance.[15]

Graglia and Wolters maintain that the Supreme Court should have known that white parents would never submit to having their children bused into black neighborhoods to attend school with black children as long as they had other options. White flight, therefore, was inevitable. They insist that the courts erred in abandoning freedom of choice plans (which were color neutral) in favor of busing plans designed to achieve a racial balance (which were color conscious and, in their words "racially discriminatory").[16] The busing debacle, they continue, is a perfect example of what can happen when the judiciary assumes legislative prerogatives belonging to Congress, whose members are elected by and directly responsible to their constituents. They conclude by arguing that busing's only accomplishment was to accelerate white flight to the suburbs, and that freedom of choice, had it been allowed to remain an option, would have worked eventually. I strongly disagree.

While it is painfully evident that busing in Richmond was a failure, it was not necessarily ill-advised, given the extent of residential segregation in the city. Under the circumstances, Judge Merhige was totally justified in ordering busing for the city. Without judicial prodding, freedom of choice would never have worked because, as has already been shown, white parents who would not freely choose yellow buses for their children could hardly be expected to choose black schools for them. It is unfortunate that Graglia and Wolters condemn racial separation only when it is mandatorily imposed, and not when it is voluntarily chosen, which amounts to an acceptance, if not an outright endorsement, of de facto segregation. Further, their characterization of busing as racial discrimination is not only grossly misleading but an unconscionable exaggeration, especially when viewed against the backdrop of this nation's history of racial discrimination against its nonwhite citizens.[17]

Although Wolters concludes that "integration has been a failure in four of the five *Brown* school districts [with the exception of Topeka]," his own assessment of the current situation in Prince Edward County contradicts him. Wolters also observes:

> Despite the problems, the 1970s witnessed a significant growth in community support for the public schools. More blacks were voting, although the percentage of blacks living in the county declined from 45 in 1950 to 38 in 1980, and whites who sent their children to public schools naturally joined with blacks in support of public education. . . .
>
> The influence of the public school coalition became apparent in November 1979. For decades the local Board of Education had been appointed by the School Trustee Electoral Board. But advocates of public education were angered during the summer of 1979 when the judge of the local circuit court appointed two well-known partisans of the Academy [Prince Edward's private school] to the Electoral Board. Parents of public school students responded by initiating a referendum providing that henceforth members of the school board should be appointed by the elected Board of Supervisors. The referendum passed easily, receiving a majority of the votes in each of the county's election districts. The same election saw the defeat of the white chairman of the Board of Supervisors, who had long been associated with the Academy, and the election of James Ghee [a local black civil–rights attorney] (who had drafted the referendum) and of two other blacks. The 1979 election indicated that public schools enjoyed broad support in the county.[18]

Apparently, neither public education nor school desegregation in Prince Edward County is as endangered as Wolters suggests.[19]

The situation in Richmond is less encouraging. There, school desegregation must be viewed within the context of geographic realities; easy access to white school systems in neighboring counties no doubt hampered desegregation efforts in Richmond (an increasingly common scenario in other large metropolitan areas, such as Atlanta, where the public schools are nearly 90 percent black). Had the United States Supreme Court upheld Judge Merhige's consolidation order in 1973, Richmond's story would very likely have a different ending. Indeed, school desegregation throughout the entire country might have taken a different direction. But, when civil–rights attorneys began to address the issue of metropolitan consolidation, a new conservative consensus had emerged, and support for desegregation was on the decline. President Richard M. Nixon, who had promised during the 1968 campaign that if elected he would end the war in Vietnam, end forced busing, and restore law and order, charted a more conservative course for the nation and devoted his first term in office to consolidating his political base. His appointments to the United States Supreme Court (Warren E. Burger, 1969; Harry A. Blackmun, 1970; Lewis F. Powell, Jr., and William H. Rehnquist, 1971), as well as numerous other appointments to lower courts, reflected the changing national mood. Clearly, as events of the 1970s would dramatically illustrate, the liberalism of the 1960s was no longer in vogue.

Unfortunately, school desegregation no longer seems to be a national priority. Richmond's thirty-five year struggle to desegregate its public schools has shown that the federal government (the executive and judicial branches in particular) is no longer committed to aggressive desegregation plans. The only alternative, therefore, is for Richmond's school system to focus on education rather than integration, in the hope that good schools will attract good students, which might eventually lead to greater ethnic and cultural diversity. The examples of Orangeburg, South Carolina, and Jackson, Mississippi, hold some promise for Richmond.

In 1970, court-ordered desegregation in South Carolina triggered a private, all-white network of segregation academies, which resulted in a de facto segregated educational system, with most black pupils in public schools and most white pupils in private schools. But a major state–government effort to improve the quality of public education has begun to pay dividends. About sixty programs, ranging from special programs for underprepared four-year-olds to exit exams for high school seniors, have helped the public school students in South Carolina—a state whose public schools once rivaled those of Mississippi as the nation's worst—raise their test scores from fiftieth in the nation to thirty-fifth. The better-financed public schools are now enticing white pupils and white teachers away from the financially strained private schools, where tuition has been increasing constantly. As a result, some of the private schools in South Carolina are in trouble, and several have recently closed.[20]

In Orangeburg, South Carolina, a community south of Columbia where a statue in the town square honors the Confederate dead and where three black pupils were killed by the state highway patrol in the 1960s, the public schools have attracted national acclaim for quality and innovation. The school district was 55 percent white before desegregation. In 1970, white enrollment plummeted to 20 percent. As of 1989, white enrollment had increased to 30 percent and is continuing to rise. "We are definitely seeing a change" in the racial composition of the student body, says Irene Myers, associate superintendent of the Orangeburg public schools. Ann O. Glover, headmistress at Orangeburg Prep, the city's largest private school, agrees. "Public schools have been pressured to improve. I can really see a difference in improvement. They have come a long way. . . . We have felt the effect of it."[21]

Changes in the overall racial climate have made public schools more acceptable to some white parents, which represents a major shift in ideology since the tension-filled 1970s. "The immediate response to desegregation was an us-against-them mentality on both sides," says James A. Wilsford, Orangeburg's school superintendent. But the atmosphere has gradually begun to change. "This is a new generation of people who look to the future and not to the past." Gaye Lanier, a teacher in Orangeburg's school system, sums it up best: "The white community abandoned the public schools twenty years ago. I was horrified that people felt they had to have their kids in private schools. It's completely different now. Parents recognize the quality is here."[22]

A similar trend is underway in Jackson, Mississippi. There, a growing group of parents, who have organized themselves into Parents for Public Schools, have set out to prove that white flight from urban public schools can be reversed. Dick Molpus, Mississippi's secretary of state and a founding member of the organization, sums up the group's motto: "Communities that have abandoned their public schools are dying communities."[23]

White flight from Jackson's public schools began in 1970, when the desegregation order took effect. By the fall of 1971, 11,000 white students had left the school system for private, segregated academies. Almost overnight, whites had dropped from 58 percent to 39 percent of the total public school population. And the flight continued. By 1989, whites made up only 21 percent of 33,000 public school students in Jackson.[24]

Since 1983, Parents for Public Schools has been preaching the virtues of public schools to anyone who would listen in this racially even city of 203,000. The fact that most of the members are middle–class professionals has helped them win converts, and their philosophy is grounded in economic self-interest as well as in morality. "It doesn't make economic sense for people to pay property taxes and send their kids to private schools," said Tim Medley, an investment adviser who is the group's president. Apparently, the group's message is catching on. White enrollment in the public schools is gradually increasing, and the organization has doubled its membership in the past six months to five hundred people. The group's members are not surprised that they are getting calls from all across the country. "Parents for Public Schools is the most powerful public school idea I've ever been associated with," said Dick Molpus, who helped

Governor William Winter pass a package of education reforms in 1982.
"This is touching the very heart of public education in American life, which
is parental and community involvement with schools." That involvement
had been missing for a long time.[25]

Whether Richmond's public schools can make a similar comeback is
uncertain. There are too many variables to be considered. If we learned
any lessons at all from the 1970s, we learned that there are limits to what
the courts can mandate, and that school desegregation, if it is to proceed
smoothly, must have the support of ordinary men and women, black and
white, working together to find common ground. We must also understand
that no matter how hopeless and depressing the situation in some inner–city
school districts may seem, we simply cannot cut them off from the rest of
society and contemptuously discard them as "superfluous appendages."[26]
What affects one of us ultimately affects all of us, and if inner city schools,
plagued by poverty and underachievement, are left to stew in their own
juices, then it will only be a matter of time before the bitter broth spills over
to the rest of the nation, manifesting itself in hatred and resentment. Let us
hope that all people of good will can work together to solve this problem
before it is too late.

Prior to the *Brown* decision, black and white children attended racially
segregated schools in Richmond. Thirty-five years later, one finds that the
scenario has changed very little: Richmond's public schools, as of this
writing, are 88 percent black. Despite the legal demise of separate but
equal education, segregated classrooms are still commonplace in
Richmond, the only difference being that the city's blacks have now been
joined by poorer white classmates whose parents lack the financial where-
withal to exercise other options. Whatever their motives, thousands of
whites abandoned the city's schools during the era of school desegregation,
an exodus that gained added momentum once a district–court judge ordered
crosstown busing. It is perhaps cruelly ironic that steps designed to bring
the races closer together succeeded only in driving them further apart. A
preoccupation with desegregation's means caused many to lose sight of its
end.

Blacks in Richmond, like blacks throughout the rest of the nation, had
experienced the inequities inherent in segregated education and, like all
parents, those in Richmond could only hope that the situation would
improve for their children. For some black parents, it was never really a
question of integration to the point of social interaction with whites, but
merely a matter of equal access. Alice Calloway clearly articulates this
point of view: "I pushed so hard for integration because I knew that the
city would appropriate sufficient funds for the schools as long as white
children were in them, and that my children would benefit as a result of
that. I've been around long enough to know that if the white child is there,

the money will be there."[27]

Still, there were those black parents who wanted integrated schools for their children not only because separate black schools were hampered with inferior facilities but because segregation carried with it a badge of cultural and racial inferiority, which caused black children to develop a distorted image of themselves. They saw school desegregation as a way of tearing down racial barriers that had historically consigned blacks to second-class citizenship. If blacks and whites could learn together as children, then it would be much easier for them to develop mutual respect for each other as adults. In this way, the evil of racism would be destroyed in its infancy. But somehow, the greater the efforts to fulfill the promise of *Brown,* the more ambiguous its intent became.

Whites, however, had different perceptions of school desegregation. Some, because of ingrained racial prejudice, could not even conceive of black and white children attending the same schools. For them, the social intimacy that would be the inevitable result was repugnant. Even those who accepted integration in principle rebelled at the notion of having their children bused into predominantly black neighborhoods. Some whites worried that the quality of education would decline proportionately as a school became blacker. Not wanting to be perceived as racists, these whites clamored only for a good education for their children. Yet, implicit in that assertion was the understanding that a good education could never be achieved within a predominantly black setting.

School desegregation means much more than black and white children sitting together in the classroom solely for the academic improvement of blacks. Desegregation means—or at least it should mean—that black and white children are conditioned at an early age to interact with one another on the basis of equality and mutual respect for the other's cultural heritage. Only this kind of cooperation can offer any hope that racism might one day disappear from our divided nation, a nation that the black writer James Baldwin satirically referred to as "these yet to be united states."[28]

In 1965 President Lyndon Johnson remarked:

> In the field of education, the common goal of white and Negro parents alike is the best possible education for their children. It is a national shame that the vast majority of Negro children are schooled even worse than they are fed. . . . Millions are trapped in ghettoes and shanties—discouraged and hopeless. They will be as far from sharing in the promise of America as if they inhabited another planet.
>
> Moreover, the isolation of Negro from white communities is increasing, rather than decreasing as Negroes crowd into the central cities and become a city within a city. . . . For Negro poverty is not white poverty. Many of its causes and many of its cures are the same. But there are differences. . . . These differences are not racial differences. They are solely and simply the consequence of ancient brutality, past injustice, and present prejudice. They

are anguishing to observe. For the Negro they are a constant reminder of oppression. For the white they are a constant reminder of guilt. But they must be faced and they must be dealt with and they must be overcome, if we are ever to reach the time when the only difference between Negroes and whites is the color of their skin.[29]

NOTES

BIBLIOGRAPHY

INDEX

Notes

Chapter One

1. *Brown v. Board of Education*, 347 U.S. 483 (1954).
2. Richmond *Times-Dispatch*, May 18, 1954. (Since the Richmond *Times-Dispatch* and the Richmond *News Leader* are the primary newspapers quoted from, references to them hereafter will be made only as *Times-Dispatch* and *News Leader*.)
3. Ibid.
4. Ibid.
5. *News Leader*, May 18, 1954.
6. Richmond *Afro-American*, May 22, 1954; *Times-Dispatch*, May 18, 1954.
7. Richmond *Afro-American*, May 22, 1954.
8. Benjamin Muse, *Virginia's Massive Resistance*, p. 7; J. Harvie Wilkinson III, *Harry Byrd and the Changing Face of Virginia Politics, 1945– 1966*, p. 118.
9. Muse, *Virginia's Massive Resistance*, p. 7.
10. *Times-Dispatch*, Aug. 29, 1954.
11. Robbins L. Gates, *The Making of Massive Resistance*, pp. 34–36. See also Numan V. Bartley, *The Rise of Massive Resistance*.
12. *Brown v. Board of Education*, 349 U.S. 294, 301 (1955).
13. The text of the Gray Commission's report is reprinted as Senate Document no. 1, Extra Session 1955, General Assembly of Virginia. A full reprint also appears in *Race Relations Law Reporter* 1 (Feb. 1956): 241 ff., Quoted in Wilkinson, *Harry Byrd*, p. 125.
14. Muse, *Virginia's Massive Resistance*, p. 16; Gates, *The Making of Massive Resistance*, pp. 62–65.
15. Wilkinson, *Harry Byrd*, p. 127.
16. *News Leader*, Nov. 21, 1955, to Feb. 2, 1956.
17. In the summer of 1989 I attempted to interview Mr. Kilpatrick regarding his position during Virginia's school desegregation crisis, but he pleaded "res ipsa loquitor" and graciously refused my request. For a more detailed examination of Kilpatrick's views and his influence in Virginia politics, see Robert Gaines Corley, "James Jackson Kilpatrick: The Evolution of a Southern Conservative, 1955– 1965," M.A. thesis, University of Virginia, 1971.
18. *Journal of the Senate of Virginia*, 1956, p. 146, quoted in Wilkinson, *Harry Byrd and the Changing Face of Virginia Politics*, p. 129.
19. New York *Times*, Feb. 26, 1956. See also Muse, *Virginia's Massive Resistance*, p. 22.
20. Gates, *The Making of Massive Resistance*, p. 123; James W. Ely, *The Crisis of*

Conservative Virginia, p. 43.

21. Muse, *Virginia's Massive Resistance*, pp. 27–28.

22. For a more thorough discussion of the enactment of the massive–resistance legislation, see Gates, *The Making of Massive Resistance*, pp. 167–90.

23. *Times-Dispatch*, Sept. 5, 1956.

24. Walter F. Murphy, "The South Counterattacks: The Anti-NAACP Laws," *Western Political Quarterly* 12 (1959): 371–90.

25. *Times-Dispatch*, Jan. 4, 1957; Ely, *The Crisis of Conservative Virginia*, p. 47.

26. Murphy, "The South Counterattacks," p. 389; Muse, *Virginia's Massive Resistance*, pp. 48–49.

27. Interview, Oliver W. Hill, June 1985.

28. *Southern School News*, Oct. 1957.

29. *Southern School News*, Apr. 1958, Oct. 1957.

30. Ibid., Oct. 1958.

31. Ibid; Muse, *Virginia's Massive Resistance*, p. 114; Wilkinson, *Harry Byrd*, p. 140.

32. Muse, *Virginia's Massive Resistance*, pp. 111–13.

33. *Harrison v. Day*, 200 Va. 439 (1959); see also *Southern School News*, Feb. 1959.

34. *James v. Almond*, 170 F. Supp. 331 (1959), 337–38.

35. *Times-Dispatch*, Jan. 21, 1959.

36. Ibid., Feb. 3, 1959.

37. Robert Collins (Bob) Smith, *They Closed Their Schools*, pp. 151–70; Gates, *The Making of Massive Resistance*, pp. 211–13; *Times-Dispatch*, Aug. 25, 1961.

38. *Griffin et al. v. County School Board of Prince Edward County et al.*, 317 U.S. 218.

39. Wilkinson, *Harry Byrd*, pp. 126–27; Gates, *The Making of Massive Resistance*, pp. 96–99. Gates divides Virginia's leaders into four different groups based on their different attitudes towards school integration. (1) *Defiant segregationists* strongly objected to any mixing of the races in public education at any time in the foreseeable future. Notables personally identified with this attitude included U.S. Representatives William M. Tuck and Watkins Abbitt, U.S. Senator Harry F. Byrd, Sr., Governor Thomas B. Stanley, and editors James J. Kilpatrick (Richmond *News Leader*) and J. Barrye Wall (Farmville *Herald*); (2) *Cushioning segregationists* preferred the separation of the races in public education and sought to "cushion" the impact of integration through a pupil–assignment plan coupled with tuition grants. Although bitterly disappointed with the *Brown* decision, they appeared to accept its legality and conceded that some compliance with the decision would come eventually. Ex-Governors John S. Battle and Colgate W. Darden, and Richmond *Times-Dispatch* editor Virginius Dabney were identified with this attitude; (3) *Public–school savers* believed that integration could be kept very limited by operating a pupil–assignment plan and tended to oppose tuition grants. State representatives Armistead Boothe and Ted Dalton were most closely associated with this group; (4) *Integrationists* felt that the abolition of segregated public education was long overdue. They accepted the legality of *Brown* and felt that it should be complied with faithfully. The NAACP, the Virginia Council on Human Relations, and some church leaders spoke in behalf of these attitudes.

40. Quoted in Ely, *The Crisis of Conservative Virginia*, p. 132.

41. Muse, *Virginia's Massive Resistance*, p. 163.

42. Wilkinson, *Harry Byrd*, p. 151.

43. Ibid., p. 152; W. G. Harris, Jr., "J. Lindsay Almond, Jr., and the Politics of School Desegregation in Virginia, 1954–1959" honors paper, Yale University, 1966, p. 22, quoted in Wilkinson, *Harry Byrd*, p. 113.

44. *Times-Dispatch*, May 7, 1959; see also Raymond Wolters, *The Burden of Brown*, p. 93.

45. Christopher Silver, *Twentieth-Century Richmond*, p. 31. Silver's study of twentieth-century Richmond provides a thorough examination of the city's history of segregated housing and the lengths that city planners went to in order to perpetuate racial separation and to ensure continued white hegemony in political and economic matters. He also discusses in detail the principal causes of "white flight" to the suburbs.

46. In 1917 the United States Supreme Court, in *Buchanan v. Warley* [245 U.S. 60 (1917)], ruled that municipal ordinances violated the Fourteenth Amendment because they were a type of overt racial discrimination by the state; restrictive covenants, however, were private contractual agreements between individuals that, though discriminatory, did not violate the Fourteenth Amendment, and they were upheld by the Court in 1926 in *Corrigan v. Buckley* [271 U.S. 323 (1926)]. In *Shelley v. Kraemer* [334 U.S. 1 (1948)], the Supreme Court held that while restrictive covenants were still private and legal acts of discrimination, they were unenforceable by resort to the courts. Though the *Corrigan* decision was not overturned, it was severely weakened.

47. Silver, *Twentieth-Century Richmond*, p. 13.

48. Ibid., pp. 106–09.

49. Civil Rights Act of 1968, quoted in *Bradley v. Richmond School Board*, 317 F. Supp. 555–61 (ED Va. 1970), (Hereafter referred to as *Bradley*.)

50. Oliver W. Hill interview. After the Supreme Court's ruling in *Shelley v. Kraemer* (see note 46, above), blacks began to challenge restrictive covenants more directly. The results were significant. In Chicago, for example, it was estimated by the local commission on human relations that within four years of the *Shelley* decision, 21,000 black families purchased or rented homes in areas formerly barred to them. Similar results could be found in Richmond. (See Richard Kluger, *Simple Justice*, p. 255.)

51. Interview, George L. Jones, Mar. 28, 1985.

52. Interview, Nathaniel Lee, May 28, 1985. Some school officials have specu-lated that overcrowding became a major problem in so many of Richmond's schools for the same reason it became a problem in many other southern school districts—a slowdown in school construction owing to uncertainty as to how the Supreme Court would rule on the pending school–desegregation suits. Also, the *Times-Dispatch* reported that along with the 3,115 students on double shift in nine Negro schools, there were also 1,643 pupils on double shift in eight of the city's white schools. See *Times-Dispatch*, May 18, 1954, p. 7.

53. Oliver W. Hill interview. See also Kluger, *Simple Justice*, pp. 214–17. Kluger's masterfully written work, which is a history of the five individual cases that were consolidated under one title and became known collectively as *Brown v.*

Board of Education, is by far the most comprehensive study of school desegrega-
tion yet to appear. Diligently researched and eloquently written, *Simple Justice* is
indispensable for students seeking a better understanding of race relations in the
United States.
54. The NAACP's first major victory in school desegregation came in 1936 in
Pearson v. Murray, 169 Md. 478, 182 A. 590 (1936). In that case, the Maryland
Court of Appeals affirmed a lower–court decision ordering the admission of Donald
Murray, a black applicant, into the University of Maryland's Law School. (Like
many southern states, Maryland refused to admit blacks into its universities, but did
operate an out-of-state scholarship program that would pay the tuition for any black
wishing to attend a black university outside the state. This policy usually affected
graduate schools, because although a state might operate black colleges, these
colleges might not offer advanced degrees.) The U.S. Supreme Court relied on the
Murray decision when it ruled in *Missouri ex rel. Gaines v. Canada*, 305 U.S. 337
(1938), that a black applicant, Lloyd Gaines, had to be admitted to the University of
Missouri's law school. The Court held: "Manifestly, the obligation of the State to
give the protection of equal laws can be performed only where its laws operate, that
is, within its own jurisdiction." Missouri could not simply satisfy its obligation by
casting it upon another state. But, the Supreme Court took an interesting twist in
Sipuel v. Oklahoma State Board of Regents, 332 U.S. 631 (1948). The Court ruled
that Oklahoma had to provide Ada Sipuel, a black applicant to the University of
Oklahoma Law School, with a legal education "in conformity with the equal
protection clause of the Fourteenth Amendment and provide it as soon as it does for
applicants of any other group." The Court remanded the case to the Oklahoma
Supreme Court, which ordered the university either to admit Miss Sipuel to the
white law school or to open up a separate one for her. The Oklahoma Board of
Regents promptly created a separate law school overnight by roping off a small
section of the state capital in Oklahoma City and reserving it for black students
only. Three law teachers were assigned to instruct Miss Sipuel and others similarly
situated. Thurgood Marshall went back to the U.S. Supreme Court to protest
Oklahoma's actions. But the high court ruled that the Oklahoma courts had not
acted in defiance of the Supreme Court's earlier decision nor had the university in
setting up its roped-off "law school" in the state capital. Hence, *Plessy v.
Ferguson*, the 1896 Supreme Court case that sanctioned "separate but equal,"was
still the law. It was not until two years later in *Sweatt v. Painter*, 210 S.W. 2d 442
(1947), 339 U.S. 629 (1950), and *McLaurin v. Oklahoma State Regents for Higher
Education*, 339 U.S. 637 (1950), that the Supreme Court began to retreat from
Plessy. See Mark V. Tushnet, *The NAACP'S Legal Strategy against Segregated
Education, 1925–1950*.
55. Hill interview.
56. For an excellent account of the evolution of NAACP legal strategy concerning
school desegregation, see Tushnet, *The NAACP's Legal Strategy against Segregated Education, 1925-1950*.
57. *Times-Dispatch*, Apr. 27, 1951.
58. Oliver W. Hill interview. I have also benefited greatly from a series of
interviews with Mr. Hill conducted by Judge A. Leon Higgenbotham at the
University of Virginia Law School television studio on April 28, 1984. These were

made available courtesy of Professor William A. Elwood, the Carter G. Woodson Institute for Afro-American and African Studies, and the Center for the Study of Civil Rights.

59. Hill was elected to Richmond's city council in 1948, but was defeated in a reelection bid in 1950. Richmond's city council would then remain all-white until the election of black real estate broker Bernard A. Cephas in 1964.

60. Richmond *Afro-American*, Aug. 19, 1950.

61. *Statistical Reports of the Richmond Public Schools*, 1950–53.

62. Richmond *Afro-American*, Aug. 15, 1953.

63. Richmond *School Board Minutes*, Aug. 27, 1956, p. 267.

Chapter Two

1. *Times-Dispatch*, Dec. 26, 1956; *Southern School News*, Jan. 1957.

2. *Southern School News*, Mar. 1957; interview, Alice R. Calloway, June 16, 1986.

3. *Times-Dispatch*, Dec. 27, 1956.

4. Statement of the Pupil Placement Board, Commonwealth of Virginia, Aug. 5, 1957, Richmond School Board.

5. *Southern School News*, June 1957; *Times-Dispatch*, Sept. 18, 1957.

6. Alice R. Calloway interview.

7. *News Leader*, Sept. 13, 1957.

8. *Times-Dispatch*, Sept. 18, 1957.

9. Richmond *School Board Minutes*, July 17, 1958; *Times-Dispatch*, July 25, 1858; *Southern School News*, Aug. 1958;

10. *Warden v. Richmond School Board* 6 Race Relations Law Reporter 1025 (ED Va. 1961).

11. *Southern School News*, June 1959; *Times-Dispatch*, Aug. 30 and Sept. 3, 1958. This suit was finally decided on July 5, 1961. The district court ordered that the one remaining Negro plaintiff be transferred from the Negro school located five miles from her home and admitted to the white school in her neighborhood. However, the court denied class relief, stating: "There is no question as to the right of the infant plaintiff to be admitted to the Schools of the City of Richmond without discrimination on the ground of race. She is admitted, however, as an individual, not as a class or group; and it is as an individual that her rights under the Constitution are asserted." The court refused to grant a permanent injunction and dismissed the case from the docket. See *Warden v. Richmond School Board*, 6 Race Relations Law Reporter 1025 (ED Va. 1961).

12. *Southern School News*, July 1960.

13. Ibid., Aug. 1960, p. 10.

14. Ibid., Sept. 1960, p. 5; *Times-Dispatch*, Sept. 7, 1960. Chandler Junior High had been the center of controversy earlier in the year. The school board had planned to convert the school from white to Negro use, but in April the board voted to continue it as a white school during the 1960–61 year. The board explained its reversal by saying that the white residents of the area had expressed "overwhelming

sentiment" against the conversion.

15. *Southern School News*, Apr., Sept. 1960.

16. Alice R. Calloway Interview.

17. *Southern School News*, Oct. 1960.

18. Alice R. Calloway interview.

19. *Bradley*, 338 F. Supp. 67, 72-73 (1972).

20. *News Leader*, Feb. 16, 1955.

21. Ely, *The Crisis of Conservative Virginia*, p. 36.

22. *Times-Dispatch*, Aug. 30, 1956, quoted in Gates, *The Making of Massive Resistance*, p. 172.

23. Speech by Byrd at Berryville, Va., Aug. 29, 1959, quoted in Ely, *The Crisis of Conservative Virginia*, p. 96; Almond quoted in Charlottesville *Daily Progress*, July 25, 1958; Wilkins quoted in Wolters, *The Burden of Brown*, p. 86.

24. *Times-Dispatch*, Mar. 26, 1957; Almond quoted in Ely, *The Crisis of Conservative Virginia*, p. 97.

25. Byrd quoted in Ely, *The Crisis of Conservative Virginia*, p. 97.

26. Richmond *School Board Minutes*, May 7, 1959, p. 258.

27. Ibid., May 15, 1961, p. 56.

28. Ibid., July 27, 1961, p. 343.

29. *Bradley*, 317 F. 2d 429 (CA 1963).

30. *Bradley*, 416 U.S. 696-99 (1962).

31. *Bradley*, 317 F. 2d 438 (CA 1963).

32. Interview, Kenneth E. Whitlock, Jr., Feb. 11, 1986.

33. Ibid.

34. Interview, Virginia Crockford, Aug. 21, 1986.

35. George L. Jones interview. Mr. Bradshaw died in 1984.

36. Interview, Lewis F. Powell, Jr., Oct. 1, 1986. I am also grateful to Justice Powell for sharing with me other pertinent information contained in his private papers.

37. Ibid.

38. Lewis Powell interview. See also Lewis F. Powell, Jr., "Reflections," *Virginia Magazine of History and Biography* 96 (1988): 322.

39. Powell to Murrow, quoted in Ann M. Sperber, *Murrow: His Life and Times* (New York: Freundlich, 1986), p. 545.

40. Lewis Powell interview.

41. "A Tribute to Justice Lewis F. Powell, Jr.," *Harvard Law Review* 101(1987): 415-16.

42. *Bradley*, 317 F. 2d 429, 435-36 (CA 1963); see also "Hearings Before the Committee on the Judiciary United States Senate, Ninety-Second Congress, Nominations of William H. Rehnquist, of Arizona, and Lewis F. Powell, Jr., of Virginia, To Be Associate Justices of the Supreme Court of the United States," Washington, D.C., 1971, p. 382.

43. Wilkins quoted in *Southern School News*, Nov. 1963.

44. *Times-Dispatch*, Mar. 19, 1963.

45. Ibid.

46. Ibid.

47. *Bradley*, 345 F. 2d 310 (1965).

48. Civil Rights Act of 1964, Title IV, Section 407(a) (2), 42 U.S.C. Section 2000c-6(a).
49. J. Harvie Wilkinson III, *From Brown to Bakke,* pp. 103-4.
50. *Bradley,* 382 U.S. 103-5 (1965); *Rogers v. Paul,* 382 U.S. 198, 200 (1965).
51. "Resolution of the School Board of the City of Richmond" (filed Mar. 30, 1966), pp. 20a, 21a, City Hall, Richmond, Va.

Chapter Three

1. *News Leader,* June 22, 1966.
2. *School Board Minutes,* Mar. 24, 1966, p. 281.
3. *Times-Dispatch,* Mar. 31, 1966.
4. *Times-Dispatch,* Apr. 22, 1966; Gates, *The Making of Massive Resistance,* p. 174.
5. *School Desegregation in Southern and Border States* (formerly *Southern School News,*), Sept. 1966, p. Va.-3.
6. Ibid., October 1966, p. A-3.
7. Interview, Dr. Francis M. Foster, Sr., Sept. 18, 1986.
8. Oliver W. Hill interview.
9. *Bradley,* 317 F. Supp. 555, 561 (1970).
10. Ibid.
11. Dr. Francis M. Foster, Sr., interview.
12. *Times-Dispatch,* Nov. 16, 1966.
13. *Implications And Recommendations of Urban Team Study on Northside Schools* November 1968; (hereafter cited as the Sartain Report), quoted in Richmond *School Board Minutes,* Nov. 21, 1968, pp. 347–49. See also the James A. Sartain Papers, Virginia Historical Society, Richmond, Va. The other members of the team were Roscoe E. Reeve, Robert K. Roney, William H. Leftwich, and Charles M. Achilles.
14. Ibid.
15. Ibid. See also *Times-Dispatch,* Nov. 22, 1968.
16. *Green v. County School Board of New Kent County,* 391 U.S. 430, 439–41 (1968).
17. Ibid.
18. *Bradley,* 317 F. Supp. 560 (ED Va. 1970).
19. *News Leader,* May 12, 1970.
20. *City of Richmond v. United States,* 422 U.S. 358 (1974).
21. *Hearings Before the Subcommittee on Civil and Constitutional Rights of the Committee on the Judiciary, House of Representatives, Ninety-Seventh Congress, First Session* on "Extension of the Voting Rights Act," Serial no. 24, Part 1 (H521-8.8), May 20, 1981, pp. 365-401. For a detailed account of Richmond's 1970 annexation of portions of Chesterfield County, see John V. Moeser and Rutledge M. Dennis, *The Politics of Annexation.*
22. *City of Richmond, Virginia v. United States,* 95(A) S. Ct. 2296 (1975) at 2309. See also *City of Richmond v. United States,* 376 F. Supp. 1344 (DC 1974).
    On June 24, 1975, the Supreme Court handed down a decision in the

Richmond annexation case. By a vote of five to three (Justice Powell did not participate), the Court rendered a decision that enabled all parties to claim a victory of sorts. Writing for the majority, Justice Byron R. White held "that an annexation reducing the relative political strength of the minority race in the enlarged city as compared with what it was before the annexation is not a statutory violation as long as the postannexation electoral system fairly recognizes the minority's political potential." The Court relied heavily on *City of Petersburg v. United States* [345 F. Supp. 1021 (1972)] in framing its opinion. In that case, the Supreme Court affirmed a lower–court ruling that the solution for Petersburg's annexation that had the effect of diluting black votes was the adoption of a ward system. What is significant about the Supreme Court ruling in the Richmond case is that while it was a five–to–three decision, all eight justices agreed that Richmond's annexation was racially motivated. The majority found that "the annexation, as it went forward in 1969, was infected by the impermissible purpose of denying the right to vote based on race through perpetuating white majority power to exclude Negroes from office through at–large elections." Justice William J. Brennan, representing Justices William O. Douglas and Thurgood Marshall in a minority opinion, filed a strong dissent. See *City of Richmond, Virginia v. United States*, 95(A) S. Ct. 2296 (1975) 2307, 2304, 2305, 2309. See also Moeser and Dennis, *The Politics of Annexation*, p. 172.

23. *Bradley*, 317 F. Supp. 566 (ED Va. 1970).

24. Ibid., pp. 572–73.

25. *News Leader*, Sept. 2, 1970; *Times-Dispatch*, Sept. 3, 1970. These enrollment projections included an additional 8,017 white students from the annexed area of Chesterfield County.

26. In 1969, Richmond's schools were 70.5 percent black. After the annexation of portions of Chesterfield, however, blacks made up 60 percent of the school population, as indicated by projected enrollment figures released in May 1970. But, since nearly five thousand white students never showed up for classes during the 1970-71 school year, the black percentage of the total enrollment quickly jumped to 65 percent.

27. *News Leader*, Nov. 12, 1970.

28. *News Leader*, Sept. 1, 1970.

29. Ibid.

30. *Times-Dispatch*, Sept. 18, 1970.

31. Ibid.

32. Motion filed by the School Board of the City of Richmond, Nov. 4, 1970, Richmond Public Schools, Richmond, Va.

33. *Bradley*, 325 F. Supp. 834 (ED Va. 1972).

34. *Times-Dispatch*, Dec. 8, 1970.

35. *Swann v. Charlotte-Mecklenburg Board of Education*, 431 F. 2d 138 (CA4 1970), affirmed as modified, 402 U.S. 1 (1971).

36. *Bradley*, 325 F. Supp. 831, 834, 847 (ED Va. 1972).

37. Ibid., p. 828. In 1971, blacks accounted for 53 percent of Richmond's school teachers, while whites accounted for 47 percent.

Chapter Four

1. *Swann v. Charlotte-Mecklenburg Board of Education*, 431 F. 2d 138 (CA 1970), affirmed as modified, 402 U.S. 1, 28, 30 (1971).
2. *Bradley*, 325 F. Supp. 828 (ED Va. 1971).
3. *News Leader*, Apr. 6, 1971.
4. See the letter submitted by Henry E. Garrett, past president of the American Psychological Association, to the *Times-Dispatch*, July 17, 1970. See also the *News Leader*'s editorial page from Nov. 21, 1955, to Feb. 2, 1956.
5. Interview, Henry L. Marsh III, Nov. 1980; George L. Jones interview. See also Maurice Duke and Daniel P. Jordan, eds., *A Richmond Reader*, pp. 408–10.
6. I have benefited greatly from the A. Jarrell Raper Papers, made available to me courtesy of Mrs. Gwynn Litchfield.
7. Holton's children were assigned to their schools under the interim desegregation plan (Plan II), which went into effect in the fall of 1970.
8. Interview, Linwood Holton, Jan. 1987.
9. Ibid.
10. Ibid.
11. *Times-Dispatch*, June 25, 1989. See also editorial, *Times-Dispatch*, Oct. 24, 1971; editorial, Richmond *Afro-American*, Jan. 16, 1971; "Holton's Achievement: Building Bridges between Virginia People," Washington *Post*, Jan. 2, 1974; "Decency and Loyalty: Linwood Holton Learns the President's Views," *Washington Monthly*, Apr. 1973, p. 48; *Time*, Nov. 15, 1971, p. 59.
12. Quoted from Gary C. Leedes and James M. O'Fallon, "School Desegregation in Richmond: A Case History," in *University of Richmond Law Review* 10 (Fall 1975-76): 1–61 (emphasis supplied). From 1940 to 1970, the black population fell from 20 percent to 11.5 percent in Chesterfield, and from 16.6 percent to 6.8 percent in Henrico. Despite annexation of a 97–percent–white portion of Chesterfield in 1970, the percentage of blacks in Richmond increased from 31.8 percent to 42.3 percent for the same years. During this period, the percentage of blacks in the entire metropolitan area (which includes Henrico and Chesterfield counties as well as the city of Richmond) remained remarkably stable; 28 percent in 1940, 26 percent in 1970. See *Bradley*, 338 F. Supp. 67 (ED Va. 1972).
13. Sartain Report, pp. 17, 18, 35.
14. Interview, Marsha Vandervall, Aug. 22, 1986.
15. Virginia Crockford interview.
16. Ibid.
17. Interview, George H. Johnson, May 1985.
18. Quoted in Robert P. Hilldrup Papers, Virginia Historical Society, Richmond, Va. Hilldrup served as the director of Public Information for the Richmond Public Schools from 1969 until 1980.
19. *Bradley*, 338 F. Supp. 67 (1972) 67–71.
20. James A. Sartain and Rutledge M. Dennis, "Richmond, Virginia: Massive Resistance without Violence," pp. 227–29, quoted in Charles V. Willie and Susan L. Greenblatt, eds., *Community Politics and Educational Change* (New York: Longman, 1981), pp. 208–36.
21. Interview, Charles Cox, Mar. 1987.

22. *Bradley*, 338 F. Supp. 67 (ED Va. 1972).

23. *Bradley*, 338 F. Supp. 84–85, 94, 244–45 (ED Va. 1972).

24. *News Leader*, Jan. 11, 1972. The defendants in the *Bradley* case made several unsuccessful attempts to force Merhige to disqualify himself from the case because of bias, but Merhige steadfastly refused, insisting that the issues involved were too important and too complex to be arbitrarily assigned to some other judge less familiar with the case.

25. Ibid., Oct. 22, 1971; *Times-Dispatch*, Feb. 18, 1972.

26. *Times-Dispatch*, Jan.. 11, 1972.

27. Ibid.

28. Hilldrup Papers.

29. Interview, Robert R. Merhige, Jr., Apr. 1987. See also Ronald J. Bacigal and Margaret I. Bacigal, "A Case Study of the Federal Judiciary's Role in Court-Ordered Busing: The Professional and Personal Experiences of U.S. District Judge Robert R. Merhige, Jr.," p. 709. In a 1986 interview, attorney Samuel W. Tucker remembered that Merhige "caught a lot of flack because he was viewed as a traitor to the white community," but that the situation was a lot worse for him and his colleague Oliver Hill, who could not count on the police protection afforded Merhige. "I'll tell you that it was no picnic being viewed as the 'uppity nigger lawyers' who started all the fuss. A cross was burned on Oliver's lawn, and he just called the fire department and went back to sleep. Oliver and I both learned to be leery of the police department because you never knew how many policemen were members of the Ku Klux Klan. We were compelled to handle the harassment ourselves. There was one period where I got a death threat over the phone every night at 2 A.M. The loss of sleep was worse than the threat. I refused to get an unlisted number, and I knew the police wouldn't do much to help. It took me quite a while to figure out how a lone black man could exert any power to stop these phone calls. Finally one night I told the caller, 'You know, if I can't get any sleep I'll have to do something else with my nights. Let me tell you all the fun things me and your mama could be doing right now.' I was never prosecuted for making an obscene phone call, and I never heard from that guy again" (interview with Samuel W. Tucker, Mar. 1986, quoted in Bacigal and Bacigal, "A Case Study," p. 711, n. 49).

30. *Bradley*, 338 F. Supp., 94–95, 118–19.

31. Bacigal and Bacigal, "A Case Study," p. 720.

32. Ibid., p. 694.

33. *Bradley*, 462 F. 2d 1058 (CA 1972).

34. *Bradley*, 462 F. 2d 1058, 1065–66, 1070 (CA 1972). In a dissenting opinion, Judge Harrison L. Winter asserted that Henrico County's schools, 89.6 percent white in 1954, were 91.9 percent white in 1971, and that Chesterfield County's schools, 79.6 percent white in 1954, were 90.6 percent white in 1971.

35. *Richmond School Board v. Virginia State Board of Education*, 412 U.S. 92 (1973).

Chapter Five

1. Although the Court's ruling in *Bradley* the previous year had been a setback for

the plaintiffs in Richmond, the vote was four to four (with Justice Powell abstaining). Thus, no clear-cut consensus emerged until *Milliken*.

2. *Milliken v. Bradley*, 418 U.S. 782.

3. Interview, Arnold R. Henderson, Jr., Aug. 1986.

4. Interview, Herman L. Carter, Jr., May 1985.

5. Interview, Angelo Setien, May 1985.

6. Marsha Vandervall interview.

7. Herman L. Carter, Jr., interview.

8. Interview, James W. Tyler, Apr. 1985.

9. Herman L. Carter, Jr., interview.

10. George H. Johnson interview.

11. Angelo Setien interview. George Wythe High School was one of the few city schools that maintained a fairly high white percentage during the 1970s.

12. George H. Johnson interview.

13. When Richard Hunter's plan was first implemented, there were still a few elementary schools (especially those in the annexed area) with a significant white enrollment. Other elementary schools across town were almost all black.

14. Richmond has long had a private school tradition, as many are quick to point out, so it is important to make the distinction between the traditional private schools, most of which still exist, and the segregationist academies, most of which have long since perished. It is very difficult to obtain extensive information on the operation of Richmond's private schools, since there is no central administration that provides information to the public. The material presented here and elsewhere throughout the text concerning private schools has been pieced together from personal interviews and enrollment figures provided by some of Richmond's private schools.

15. Interview, Richard C. Hunter, Mar. 1983.

16. James. W. Tyler interview.

17. Statistics made available by Richmond's Department of Planning and Development, City Hall. See also *News Leader*, Aug. 30, 1986.

18. Comments made by Nathaniel Lee at a symposium entitled "Schools, Public Education, and Race," held at the Valentine Museum, Apr. 20, 1986.

19. *Times-Dispatch*, June 12, 1990.

20. Ibid.

21. Ibid. Lucille Brown replaced Albert Jones as superintendent in 1991.

22. Ibid; Melvin Law interview.

23. *Bradley v. Baliles*, 639 F. Supp. 680 (ED Va. 1986).

24. *Times-Dispatch*, Oct. 12, 1985, and Apr. 10, 1987.

25. *Bradley v. Baliles*, 639 F. Supp. 690.

26. *Bradley v. Baliles*, 829 Fed. Rep. 2d 1308 (CA 1987).

27. Judge Merhige tried to shed some light on the controversial funding issue by explaining the difference between *equalized* and *unequalized* funding.

> State aid to school districts is divided into two categories: equalized funding and unequalized funding. Equalized funding is allocated according to the locality's ability to raise revenues to support its schools and the number of children in the district eligible to attend school. Under this formula, then, wealthier districts receive less state aid than do poorer districts. Because

Richmond is a wealthy school district, due to its high real estate tax base, Richmond Public Schools receives a relatively low amount of equalized funding. In the 1985-86 school year, for example, Richmond received $591 per pupil in equalized state funding, while Henrico received $692 and Chesterfield received $904. The state average was $808.

In contrast to equalized funding, however, unequalized funding is distributed, not on the basis of the district's wealth, but rather on the basis of certain "programmatic data." The amount of unequalized funding that Richmond Public Schools receives exceeds both the state average and the amounts allocated to Henrico or Chesterfield. Richmond received $1,117 per pupil in the 1985–86 school year. The state average was $812, while Henrico and Chesterfield received $852 and $692, respectively.

When equalized and unequalized funding are considered together, Richmond Public Schools received more of such funding than Henrico, Chesterfield, or the state average. The state average in 1985–86 was $1,623. Richmond received $1,709, while Henrico received $1,550 and Chesterfield received $1,596.

In addition to equalized and unequalized funding, the State has also provided aid specifically for remedial education. The statistics for the six years between 1980 and 1986 are as follows:

	Richmond	Henrico	C'field
1980–81	$552,453	$39,000	$31,000
1981–82	543,003	39,000	31,000
1982–83	1,085,200	142,245	80,325
1983–84	1,132,917	145,590	82,110
1984–85	828,606	60,652	46,774
1985–86	935,504	74,340	57,330

As can be seen, Richmond Public Schools has consistently received far greater amounts of remedial funding from the State than has either Henrico or Chesterfield. It is therefore clear that the State already provides Richmond Public Schools with a disproportionately large amount of funding. . . . The Court finds that the amount provided by the State is sufficient to satisfy whatever remaining constitutional obligation the State may have. See *Bradley v. Baliles*, 639 F. Supp. 680, at 700 and 701.

28. Melvin Law interview.

Epilogue

1. In 1986 Richmond's school board adopted a new pupil–reassignment plan that reduced busing for the purpose of desegregation. The stated purpose of the new plan was "to minimize overcrowding in some buildings . . . to reduce transportation costs . . . and to maximize the neighborhood school concept." The plan would not create any "significant change in the racial composition" within the schools. (See Richmond *School Board Minutes*, Feb, 21, 1986, p. 23; Mar. 4, 1986, p. 29; and Mar. 27, 1986, p. 36.)

2. *News Leader*, Aug. 29, 1986.

3. Ibid.

4. Ibid.

5. Ibid.

6. Ibid.

7. Ibid.

8. Charles Cox interview.

9. Interview, Virginius Dabney, June 1989. See also Morton Sosna, "Virginius Dabney: Publicist for a Liberal South," in *In Search of the Silent South: Southern Liberals and the Race Issue* (New York: Columbia University Press, 1977), pp. 121–39, quoted in Duke and Jordan, eds., *A Richmond Reader*, pp. 381–97.

10. Dabney quoted in Sosna, "Virginius Dabney," p. 394.

11. Ibid. See also John T. Kneebone, *Southern Liberal Journalists and the Issue of Race*.

12. Virginius Dabney interview.

13. New York *Times*, Jan. 5, 1969.

14. Lino A. Graglia, *Disaster by Decree*, pp. 15, 17.

15. Raymond Wolters, *The Burden of Brown*, pp. 7, 8.

16. The freedom of choice option has been revived lately, with President Bush being one of its strongest advocates. See "The Fight over School Choice," in *Time*, Mar. 13, 1989, p. 54.

17. In 1966, eminent sociologist and educational researcher James S. Coleman conducted a study of the effects of integration on black and white children. Published under the title *Equality of Educational Opportunity*, but commonly referred to as the Coleman Report, the study revealed that black children's academic performance generally improved in an integrated setting. Because of this finding, Coleman was frequently called upon to offer expert testimony on the positive effects of integration, and eventually became known as "The Scholar Who Inspired Busing." In 1978, Coleman conducted a new study that contradicted his earlier findings. He conceded that integration would not necessarily improve the academic performance of lower–class blacks. In fact, the most that could be said for large–scale integration was that academic scores usually did not decline. Wolters relies upon Coleman's "revised" report to support his contention that "contrary to the expectations of those who favored desegregation, the quality of public education available to blacks is generally no better than it was in 1954" (Wolters, *The Burden of Brown*, p. 284). See James S. Coleman et al., *Equality of Educational Opportunity* (Washington, D.C.: U.S. Department of Health, Education, and Welfare, 1966). See also *National Observer*, June 7, 1975.

18. Wolters, *The Burden of Brown*, pp. 124–25, 273.

19. Wolters relies upon the *Briggs* dictum as the constitutional basis for his argument. In 1949, twenty black plaintiffs in Summerton (Clarendon County), South Carolina, filed a petition with the federal court, alleging that the white schools were vastly superior to the black schools in every conceivable way. The Reverend Joseph A. Delaine, a prominent black minister and civil–rights activist, was the lead plaintiff, and Thurgood Marshall was their attorney. When the case finally went to court in 1951, a three-judge district court ordered that the facilities be equalized, but held that racial segregation in the public schools was not in and of

itself a denial of the equal protection of the law. Writing for the court, Judge John J. Parker concluded: "It is important that we point out exactly what the Supreme Court has decided and what it has not decided. . . . all that it has decided, is that a state may not deny to any person on account of race the right to attend any school that it maintains. . . . Nothing in the Constitution or in the decision of the Supreme Court takes away from the people the freedom to choose the schools they attend. The Constitution, in other words, does not require integration. It merely forbids discrimination. It does not forbid such segregation as occurs as the result of voluntary action. It merely forbids the use of governmental power to enforce segregation." This constitutional ideology is referred to as the *Briggs* dictum. Judge George Bell Timmerman concurred with the decision. Judge J. Waties Waring, a native Charlestonian who had earlier suggested to Thurgood Marshall that the NAACP mount a direct challenge against segregation, issued a strongly worded and much–heralded dissent, in which he concluded that "segregation is per se inequality." (*Briggs v. Elliott* 98 F. Supp. 529 (1951), 103 F. Supp. 920 (1952), 347 U.S. 497 (1954), 132 F. Supp. 776 (1955): p. 777.) For a closer examination of Judge Waring and his views on racial issues, see Tinsley E. Yarbrough, *A Passion for Justice.*

20. Atlanta *Journal and Constitution*, Sept. 30, 1989.

21. Ibid.

22. Ibid.

23. Atlanta *Journal and Constitution*, Oct. 5, 1990.

24. Ibid.

25. Ibid.

26. "Superfluous appendages" has been used to describe the bantustans, or home-lands in South Africa, where most blacks are required by law to reside.

27. Alice R. Calloway interview.

28. James Baldwin as quoted by Maya Angelou in a performance at the University of Georgia, November 1988.

29. Comments made by President Lyndon B. Johnson at a White House civil rights planning session, Nov. 16, 1965, quoted in *Congressional Quarterly Weekly Report* 23, no. 48, p. 2414, and remarks made at Howard University's commencement exercises, June 4, 1965, quoted in *Congressional Quarterly Weekly Report* 23, no. 25, p. 1196.

Bibliography

Manuscript Collections
Robert P. Hilldrup Papers, Virginia Historical Society, Richmond, Va.
Lewis F. Powell, Jr. Papers (private collection)
A. Jarrell Raper Papers (private collection)
James A. Sartain Papers, Virginia Historical Society, Richmond, Va.
H. I. Willett Papers, Virginia Commonwealth University Library

Public Documents
Hearings Before the Committee on the Judiciary United States Senate, Ninety-Second Congress, Nominations of William H. Rehnquist, of Arizona, and Lewis F. Powell, Jr., of Virginia, To Be Associate Justices of the Supreme Court of the United States. Washington, D.C., 1971.
Historical Overview of the Richmond Public Schools. Richmond, Va.: Department of Community and Governmental Relations, Aug. 21, 1980.
James A. Sartain et al. *Implications and Recommendations of Urban Team Study of Northside Schools*. Submitted to Richmond Public School Board on Feb. 20, 1969.
Richmond *School Board Minutes*, Richmond Public Schools, City Hall, Richmond, Va. (1950–89).

Court Cases
Bradley v. Baliles, 639 F. Supp. 680 (ED Va. 1986).
Bradley v. Baliles, 829 Fed. Rep. 2d 1308 (CA 1987).
Bradley v. Richmond School Board, 317 F. 2d 429 (CA 1963).
Bradley v. Richmond School Board, 345 F. 2d 310 (1965).
Bradley v. Richmond School Board, 382 U.S. 103 (1965).
Bradley v. Richmond School Board, 317 F. Supp. 555 (ED Va. 1970).
Bradley v. Richmond School Board, 325 F. Supp. 828 (ED Va. 1971).
Bradley v. Richmond School Board, 338 F. Supp. 67 (ED Va. 1972).
Bradley v. Richmond School Board, 462 F. 2d 1058 (CA 1972).

Brown v. Board of Education, 347 U.S. 483 (1954).

Brown v. Board of Education, 349 U.S. 294 (1955).

City of Richmond v. United States, 376 F. Supp. 1344 (DC 1974).

City of Richmond, Virginia v. United States, 95 (A) S. Ct. 2296 (1975).

Green v. County School Board of New Kent, 391 U.S. 430 (1968).

Harrison v. Day, 200 Va. 439 (1959).

James v. Almond, 170 F. Supp. 331 (1959).

Milliken v. Bradley, 94 S. Ct. 3112 (1974).

Richmond School Board v. Virginia State Board of Education, 412 U.S. 92 (1973).

Swann v. Charlotte-Mecklenburg Board of Education, 402 U.S. 1 (1971).

Richmond *School Board Reports*, Richmond Public Schools, City Hall, Richmond, Va. (1960–69).

Hearings Before the Subcommittee on Civil and Constitutional Rights of the Committee on the Judiciary, House of Representatives, "Extension of the Voting Rights Act," Serial no. 24, Part 1 (H521-8.8), May 20, 1981, pp. 365-401.

Statistical Reports of the Richmond Public Schools. The School Board of the City of Richmond, 1950–53.

Newspapers and Magazines

Atlanta *Journal and Constitution* (1989–90)

Charlotte *Observer* (1969–71)

Charlottesville *Daily Progress* (1970)

National Observer (1975)

New York *Times* (1956, 1969–70)

Norfolk *Virginian-Pilot* (1968–71)

Richmond *Afro-American* (1950–89)

Richmond *News Leader* (1948–89)

Richmond *Times-Dispatch* (1948–89)

Southern School News (1957–65) (In 1966, the name of this publication was changed to *School Desegregation in Southern and Border States*.)

Time (1970, 1971, 1989)

Washington Monthly (1973)

Washington *Post* (1971, 1974)

Interviews (All interviews took place in Richmond, Virginia, unless otherwise noted.)

Zeke Allison (June 1989), Alice R. Calloway (June 1986), Herman L. Carter, Jr. (May 1985), Charles Cox (Mar. 1987), Virginia Crockford (Aug. 1986), Virginius Dabney (June 1989), Dr. Francis M. Foster, Sr. (Sept. 1986), Harold E. and Laura Greer (June 1987), Arnold R. Henderson, Jr. (Aug. 1986), Oliver W. Hill (June 1985), Linwood Holton (Washington,

D.C., Jan. 1987), Richard C. Hunter (Mar. 1983), George H. Johnson (May 1985), Sabrina C. Johnson (June 1989), George L. Jones, (Mar. 1985), Melvin Law (June 1990), Nathaniel Lee (May 1985), Henry L. Marsh III (Nov. 1980), Robert R. Merhige, Jr. (Apr. 1987), Lewis F. Powell, Jr. (Washington, D.C., Oct. 1986), Angelo Setien (May 1985), Samuel W. Tucker (June 1985), James W. Tyler (Apr. 1985), Bernard C. and Marsha Vandervall (Aug. 1986), Roy A. West (June 1985), and Kenneth E. Whitlock, Jr. (Feb. 1986).

Books and Articles

Bacigal, Ronald J., and Margaret I. Bacigal. "A Case Study of the Federal Judiciary's Role in Court-Ordered Busing: The Professional and Personal Experiences of U.S. District Judge Robert R. Merhige, Jr." *Journal of Law and Politics* 3 (1987): 693–725.

Bartley, Numan V. *The Rise of Massive Resistance: Race and Politics in the South during the 1950s.* Baton Rouge: Louisiana State University Press, 1969.

Boykin, Leander. "The Status and Trends of Differentials between White and Negro Teachers' Salaries in the Southern States, 1900–1946." *Journal of Negro Education* 18 (Winter 1949): 40–47.

Buni, Andrew. *The Negro in Virginia Politics, 1902–1965.* Charlottesville: University Press of Virginia, 1967.

Chafe, William H. *Civilities and Civil Rights: Greensboro, North Carolina, and the Black Struggle for Freedom.* New York and Oxford: Oxford University Press, 1980.

Dabney, Virginius. *Across the Years: Memories of a Virginian.* Garden City, N.Y.: Doubleday, 1978.

———. *Richmond: The Story of a City.* Charlottesville: University Press of Virginia, 1990.

———. *Virginia, the New Dominion: A History from 1607 to the Present.* Garden City, N.Y.: Doubleday and Company, 1971.

Dalfiume, Richard. "The 'Forgotten Years' of the Negro Revolution." *Journal of American History* 55 (June 1968): 90–106.

Doherty, James L. *Race and Education in Richmond.* Privately published in the U.S.A., 1972.

DuBois, W. E. B. "The Board of Directors on Segregation." *Crisis* 41 (May 1934): 149.

———. "Does the Negro Need Separate Schools?" *Journal of Negro Education* 4 (July 1935): 328–35.

Duke, Maurice, and Daniel P. Jordan. *A Richmond Reader, 1733–1983.* Chapel Hill: University of North Carolina Press, 1983.

Ely, James W. *The Crisis of Conservative Virginia: The Byrd Organization and the Politics of Massive Resistance.* Knoxville: University of

Tennessee Press, 1971.

Gaillard, Frye. *The Dream Long Deferred*. Chapel Hill: University of North Carolina Press, 1988.

Gates, Robbins L. *The Making of Massive Resistance: Virginia's Politics of Public School Desegregation, 1954–56*. Chapel Hill: University of North Carolina Press, 1962.

Gavins, Raymond. *The Perils and Prospects of Southern Black Leadership: Gordon Blaine Hancock, 1884–1970*. Durham, N.C.: Duke University Press, 1977.

Graglia, Lino A. *Disaster by Decree: The Supreme Court Decisions on Race and the Schools*. Ithaca, N.Y.: Cornell University Press, 1976.

Hochschild, Jennifer L. *The New American Dilemma: Liberal Democracy and School Desegregation*. New Haven, Conn.: Yale University Press, 1984.

Houston, Charles H. "Educational Inequalities Must Go!" *Crisis* 42 (Oct. 1935): 300.

Kluger, Richard. *Simple Justice: The History of Brown v. Board of Education and Black America's Struggle for Equality*. New York: Alfred A. Knopf, 1975.

Kneebone, John T. *Southern Liberal Journalists and the Issue of Race, 1920–1944*. Chapel Hill: University of North Carolina Press, 1985.

Kousser, J. Morgan. "Separate but Not Equal: The Supreme Court's First Decision on Racial Discrimination in Schools." *Journal of Southern History* 46 (Feb. 1980): 17–44.

Leedes, Gary C., and James M. O'Fallon. "School Desegregation in Richmond: A Case History." *University of Richmond Law Review* 10 (Fall 1975–76): 1–61.

Lukas, J. Anthony. *Common Ground: A Turbulent Decade in the Lives of Three American Families*. New York: Alfred A. Knopf, 1985.

McNeil, Genna Rae. "Community Initiative in the Desegregation of District of Columbia Schools, 1947–1954." *Howard Law Journal* 23 (1980): 25–41.

———. *Groundwork: Charles Hamilton Houston and the Struggle for Civil Rights*. Philadelphia: University of Pennsylvania Press, 1983.

Metcalf, George. *From Little Rock to Boston: The History of School Desegregation*. Westport, Conn.: Greenwood Press, 1983.

Moeser, John V., and Rutledge M. Dennis. *The Politics of Annexation: Oligarchic Power in a Southern City*. Cambridge, Mass.: Schenkman Publishing Company, 1982.

Murphy, Walter F. "The South Counterattacks: The Anti-NAACP Laws." *Western Political Quarterly* 12 (June 1959): 371–90.

Muse, Benjamin. *Ten Years of Prelude: The Story of Integration since the Supreme Court's 1954 decision*. New York: Viking Press, 1964.

———. *Virginia's Massive Resistance*. Bloomington: Indiana University Press, 1961.

Orfield, Gary. *Must We Bus? Segregated Schools and National Policy*. Washington, D.C.: Brookings Institution, 1978.

Pride, Richard A., and J. David Woodard. *The Burden of Busing: The Politics of Desegregation in Nashville, Tennessee*. Knoxville: University of Tennessee Press, 1985.

Ravitch, Diane. *The Troubled Crusade*. New York: Basic Books, 1983.

Rossell, Margaret. *The Carrot or the Stick for School Desegregation Policy: Magnet Schools or Forced Busing*. Philadelphia: Temple University Press, 1990.

Sartain, James A., and Rutledge M. Dennis. "Richmond, Virginia: Massive Resistance without Violence." Pp. 208-36 in *Community Politics and Educational Change*, ed. Charles V. Willie and Susan L. Greenblatt. New York: Longman, 1981.

Schwartz, Bernard. *Swann's Way: The School Busing Case and the Supreme Court*. New York: Oxford University Press, 1986.

Silver, Christopher. *Twentieth-Century Richmond: Planning, Politics, and Race*. Knoxville: University of Tennessee Press, 1984.

Smith, Robert Collins (Bob). *They Closed Their Schools: Prince Edward County, Virginia, 1951–1964*. Chapel Hill: University of North Carolina Press, 1965.

Suggs, Henry Lewis. *P. B. Young, Newspaperman: Race, Politics, and Journalism in the New South, 1910–1962*. Charlottesville: University Press of Virginia, 1988.

Thompson, Charles H. "Court Action the Only Reasonable Alternative to Remedy Immediate Abuses of the Negro Separate School." *Journal of Negro Education* 4 (Summer 1935): 433.

Tushnet, Mark V. *The NAACP's Legal Strategy against Segregated Education, 1925–1950*. Chapel Hill and London: University of North Carolina Press, 1987.

Wilkinson, J. Harvie, III. *From Brown to Bakke: The Supreme Court and School Integration, 1954–1978*. Oxford: Oxford University Press, 1979.

———. *Harry Byrd and the Changing Face of Virginia Politics, 1945–1966*. Charlottesville: University Press of Virginia, 1968.

Wolters, Raymond. *The Burden of Brown: Thirty Years of School Desegregation*. Knoxville: The University of Tennessee Press, 1984.

Woodward, Bob, and Scott Armstrong. *The Brethren: Inside the Supreme Court*. New York: Simon and Schuster, 1979.

Yarbrough, Tinsley E. *A Passion for Justice: J. Waties Waring and Civil Rights*. Oxford: Oxford University Press, 1987.

INDEX

(boldface numbers indicate a photograph)

DATE DUE

JA 78		
JAN 0 2 2010		

DEMCO 38-297